POSITIVE BUSINESS

the secrets of
SUCCESSFUL TEAM
MANAGEMENT

POSITIVE BUSINESS

the secrets of
SUCCESSFUL TEAM
MANAGEMENT

MICHAEL WEST

dbp

DUNCAN BAIRD PUBLISHERS
LONDON

The Secrets of Successful Team Management
Michael West

First published in the United Kingdom and Ireland in 2004 by
Duncan Baird Publishers Ltd
Sixth Floor
Castle House
75–76 Wells Street
London W1T 3QH

Conceived, created and designed by Duncan Baird Publishers.

Managing Editor: Judy Barratt
Editor: Lucy Latchmore
Managing Designer: Manisha Patel
Designer: Suzanne Tuhrim
Commissioned artwork: Melvyn Evans and David Dean

British Library Cataloguing-in-Publication Data:
A CIP record for this book is available from the British Library.

ISBN: 1-904292-96-8

10 9 8 7 6 5 4 3 2 1

Typeset in Bembo
Colour reproduction by Scanhouse, Malaysia
Printed in Singapore by Imago

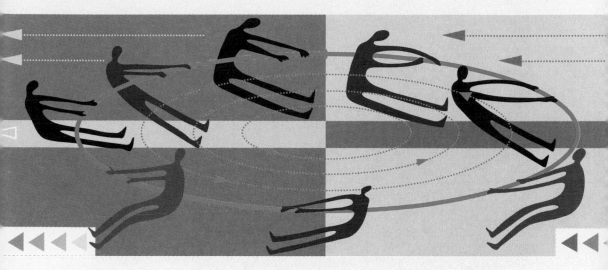

To Ellie

Evolved individuals lead others by
Opening their minds,
Reinforcing their centres,
Relaxing their desires,
Strengthening their characters

The Tao of Power
Wing (1986)

CONTENTS

AUTHOR'S INTRODUCTION   8

CHAPTER ONE: TEAMS WORK   **10**
TEAMS IN CONTEXT   12
THE BENEFITS OF TEAMWORKING   16
Work solution 1: A task for a team?   **19**
TEAM COMPETENCIES   20
Work solution 2: Assessing the competencies of your team   **23**
TYPES OF TEAMS   24
TEAM MANAGEMENT STYLES   26
THE ESSENCE OF TEAM MANAGEMENT   28

CHAPTER TWO: SELF-MANAGEMENT   **32**
TIME MANAGEMENT   34
Work solution 3: Keeping a time-management journal   **37**
SELF-AWARENESS   38
Work solution 4: Meditating into mindfulness   **41**
RECEIVING FEEDBACK   42
Work solution 5: Dealing with formal feedback   **43**
DEALING WITH NEGATIVE EMOTIONS   44
POSITIVE THINKING   46
BEING ASSERTIVE   48
Work solution 6: Dealing with difficult team members   **49**
EMPATHY AND RESONANCE   50
COMMUNICATION SKILLS   52
Work solution 7: Preparing a spoken presentation   **55**
POWER, INFLUENCE AND NETWORKING   58
Work solution 8: The art of persuasion   **61**

CHAPTER THREE: TEAM BUILDING   **62**
STAGES OF TEAM DEVELOPMENT   64
CREATING A BALANCED TEAM   66
INTERVIEWING AND RECRUITING   70
PERSONALITY AND TEAMWORK   72
FOCUS AND VALUES: CREATING A TEAM IDENTITY   74
Work solution 9: Laying down the groundrules   **77**
ESTABLISHING TEAM ROLES   78
Work solution 10: Role clarification   **79**
IMPROVING COMMUNICATION WITHIN THE TEAM   80
Work solution 11: Processing information usefully   **83**
CREATING AN ATMOSPHERE OF WARMTH AND SUPPORT   84
Work solution 12: Building two-way relationships   **85**

CHAPTER FOUR: TEAM PROCESSES   **88**
SHAPING VISION AND OBJECTIVES   90
Work solution 13: Setting objectives   **93**
MANAGING MEETINGS   94
Work solution 14: Setting an agenda   **95**
ENCOURAGING PARTICIPATION   96
Work solution 15: Step-ladder debating   **99**
CREATIVE PROBLEM-SOLVING   100
Work solution 16: Stakeholder analysis   **103**
MAKING DECISIONS   104
Work solution 17: Two-stage brainstorming   **107**
PLANNING PROCESSES AND RISK MANAGEMENT   108
Work solution 18: Managing the risks   **111**
CONDUCTING APPRAISALS   112
REWARDS AND INCENTIVES   116

CHAPTER FIVE: TEAMS IN TROUBLE   **120**
CAUSES OF FAILURE   122
DIFFICULT PEOPLE   124
INTERPERSONAL CONFLICT   126
GROUPTHINK   128
SOCIAL LOAFING   130
Work solution 19: Maximizing effort   **131**
DEFENSIVE ROUTINES   132
Work solution 20: Confronting defensive routines **135**

CHAPTER SIX: TEAMS AND THEIR ORGANIZATIONS   **136**
MOVING TOWARD TEAM-BASED WORKING   138
Work solution 21: Evaluating teamworking   **141**
INITIATING CHANGE   142
Work solution 22: Forming a change team   **143**
SEEKING ORGANIZATIONAL SUPPORT   144
EMPOWERING YOUR TEAM   146
BRIDGING BETWEEN TEAMS   148
Work solution 23: Lowering the drawbridge   **151**

REFLEXIVITY: THE KEY TO TEAM SUCCESS   152

FURTHER READING   154
INDEX   155
ACKNOWLEDGMENTS   160

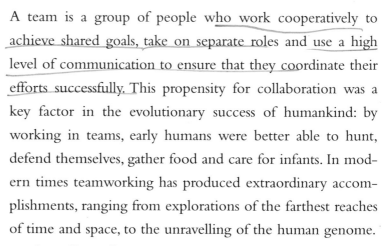

AUTHOR'S INTRODUCTION

A team is a group of people who work cooperatively to achieve shared goals, take on separate roles and use a high level of communication to ensure that they coordinate their efforts successfully. This propensity for collaboration was a key factor in the evolutionary success of humankind: by working in teams, early humans were better able to hunt, defend themselves, gather food and care for infants. In modern times teamworking has produced extraordinary accomplishments, ranging from explorations of the farthest reaches of time and space, to the unravelling of the human genome.

As well as offering us a means of progress, teams provide a domain within which we can learn and grow as members of a community: putting self-interest aside in favour of shared interests; learning to communicate effectively; helping each other out; and managing the inevitable conflicts in ways that strengthen our relationships. Working in this way we learn more than when we work alone and we also benefit from the warmth of social support. Our common experiences of living and working together bind us with each other, giving us a valued sense of belonging and a means through which to express both our collective identity and our individuality.

I first became aware of the importance of teamworking when I worked as a coal miner for a year after finishing my university education and before embarking on an academic career. In my job in the mines it quickly became clear to me that the team you worked in determined your safety underground and how effective you were in your job. This

experience led to a career-long fascination with teamworking and, in particular, with what enables teams to be creative, innovative and effective.

Since then I have studied thousands of teams in many organizational settings around the world, including aluminium smelting teams in Norway, nursing teams in Australia and postal worker teams in the Netherlands. What has consistently struck me is how effective teamworking can be in delivering complex products and services, and how little most organizations have done to develop real teamworking. The potential is enormous. However, successful teamworking requires good team management. This book aims to help team managers by offering them some simple pointers for creating and sustaining successful teams.

chapter 1

TEAMS WORK

Teams are the natural unit for all small-scale human endeavour. Our prehistoric ancestors – the hunter-gatherers – worked in teams to build communities, find food and ward off danger. There is nothing new about the team: it is a natural state of existence for a species that is inherently sociable. However, teams went out of fashion with the Industrial Revolution. It is only in the last twenty years that modern organizations have begun to appreciate the benefits that teams can bring to businesses as a whole, and to the people who work within them.

In this chapter we explore these topics in greater detail. First we look at the historical significance of teams as well as the benefits they can offer in the modern commercial world. Then we consider what makes a successful team, exploring core team skills as well as different types of teams. We also address the role of the team manager: the specific skills he or she requires to increase team competence; the different management interventions required for different types of teams; the most effective style of team management; and other important aspects of the role.

Despite our evolutionary preference for teamworking, it has only recently come back into fashion in the business world, after a long period of neglect.

Until the late 18th century most people worked in small groups practising crafts or working the land, or in businesses of fewer than 30 people. Apart from the army and the church there were few large organizations. All this changed during the Industrial Revolution, when the development of mass-production techniques sparked a dramatic shift in working practices. Industrialists began to see the profits that could accrue from producing goods in bulk rather than small batches. Cottage industries comprising small groups of people working cooperatively were replaced by efficient but dehumanizing factories in which each worker performed one highly specialized task in order to maximize productivity overall. This move toward tightly structured, mechanized methods of production culminated in the four-mile-long car-production plant of Henry Ford – a man who famously commented, in a statement that underlines the inflexibility of the assembly-line approach, that the customers could have any colour of Ford they wanted as long as it was black.

As markets became increasingly competitive, a mechanistic operation of this kind could not survive: size needed to be married with flexibility. At the same time researchers discovered that work groups had as much influence over productivity as managers. However, because there was no conduit for the exchange of skills or ideas, workers in the vast corporations were unable to contribute their knowledge of

materials, processes and working methods to the task of increasing a company's competitiveness.

Innovations in business models emerged during the reconstruction era after the Second World War. Japan led the way by applying a team ethic to the principles of mass-production. Their employees were highly motivated, committed to quality and highly productive. And the firms they worked for scared their European and US competitors into copying their ways of organizing work, while avoiding the barrier of hierarchy that inhibited innovation in Japanese culture. However, this was no easy recipe to follow; even today adopting a team approach is a challenge with which many companies struggle. The HR Directors of the top 100 US companies report that their major concern is learning to build team-based structures so that their organizations can be more flexible, productive, agile and effective.

Of course, building teams is not just about profits and innovations, it is also important for our health. When we work in teams, we have good friendships within the workplace, and we feel understood and valued. We have a sense of belonging. In today's corporate world, with its monolithic organizations, this sense of belonging can be elusive. We may feel a yawning gap between the rhetoric of the chief executive ("people are our most important asset") and the reality of our experience as employees. As a result people often feel undervalued by their employers and experience a lack of control over their work. Such alienation is compounded when companies become leaner in response to economic pressures, as this tends to result in mounting workloads and the constant threat of redundancy.

Given this environment it is hardly surprising to find that

levels of depression in Western workforces have risen dramatically over the decades – a trend that has established itself despite considerable improvements in economic prosperity. The problems caused by alienation not only harm individual employees but also affect the whole organization.

Workers who feel they don't belong are less committed to their work, less motivated to achieve, and less loyal to their company than those who have a sense of belonging. All these factors have negative implications for the overall productivity and profitability of the company. The current shift toward team-based structures represents an attempt to overcome some of these problems, in the belief that teamworking offers the promise of greater progress than can be achieved, on the one hand through individual effort, or on the other hand through mechanistic or hierarchical approaches to work.

Within the team-based model there is scope for different types of teams. In addition to traditional functional "teams" in which members have similar skills but work independently on different sets of tasks (for example, departmental teams), there are now increasing numbers of cross-functional teams. These are defined as groups of three or more people who work interdependently, combining different skills to achieve a set of mutually agreed goals. Sometimes individual team members fulfil their own role; sometimes they share a role. Sometimes work is project-based; sometimes it is ongoing. Cross-functional teams offer the most creative approach to working and it is these that form the primary focus of this book. However, most of the suggestions can be applied to all types of teams. After all, evolution has shaped us for team-work, and the basic principles have changed little since our ancestors hunted in groups on the savannah. Now as then, shared objectives, clear roles, effective communication and continual learning are the keys to team success.

THE BENEFITS OF TEAMWORKING

When we work in teams we catch more wildebeest, feel safe and have more fun. The benefits are thus both hard and soft. Below I give the main advantages, under both headings.

Hard benefits

The more teams there are in your organization, the flatter the structure should inevitably be. True teamworking means giving responsibility and authority to teams to make decisions on how to do the work in the most effective way; and this implies fewer managers and managerial levels. Decisions can be taken quickly, without passing through the links in a long hierarchical chain. Team-based organizations can therefore

respond quickly and effectively in the fast-changing environments most organizations now encounter.

Teams can *speedily develop and deliver* products. For example, in team-based car factories, workers operate in teams to assemble one car at a time from start to finish. Functioning in parallel in this way, workers can help each other in times of difficulty. This contrasts with assembly-line systems, which are only as strong as their weakest link:

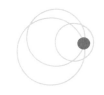

when one process in the chain breaks down, production is disrupted for all.

Teams *enable organizations to learn* (and retain learning) more effectively, because when one member leaves, the learning of the team is not lost. Cross-functional teams promote *improved quality management.* This is because a combination of different team members' perspectives (knowledge, experience, skills) will lead to questioning whether a product or a service is as good as it can be. This cross-fertilization of ideas also promotes *creativity and innovation.*

Teamwork also brings *financial benefits*, including those resulting from increased productivity. An analysis of the combined results of 131 studies of organizational change conducted in the US in 1993 found that, of all the attempts to improve company efficiency, those with the greatest positive effects upon financial performance were team-development interventions and involved the creation of self-managing teams. Another review of 12 large-scale surveys and 185 case studies of managerial practices conducted in the US in 1994 showed that team-based working led to improvements in organizational performance on measures of both *efficiency and quality.*

Change within an organization is also more effective when teamworking is already present or is a component of the change: it is easier to roll out change through ten teams of six people working together than through 60 individuals. Teams are also more likely to implement the change in a mutually agreed way, rather than idiosyncratically.

Soft benefits

For individual employees, teamworking also has real personal benefits. Employees who work in effective teams report *lower levels of stress*. This is partly because of the sense of support generated within teams as members share their struggles and successes. Stress is also reduced because team members feel much *clearer about their roles*, as team colleagues help in clarifying what those roles are. Team workers have commented on the satisfaction gained by everyone *learning from each other*, as well as on higher levels of *involvement and commitment* in their work. This latter factor can be explained by the empowerment that team members experience when, as part of a group, they have input into decisions that affect their working lives. (By contrast, most other employee involvement plans, such as quality circles, have not tended to generate a real sense of involvement.) Teamworking also makes people feel more powerful in their relationship with management, and this, of course, makes sense: if I object alone to policies, I am a single, quiet voice; if I shout in unison with team colleagues, my points are likely to be heard.

Of course, implementing teams does not automatically lead to such benefits. When teams are formed for tasks that are unsuitable for them, people fall out and the dark side of human nature emerges. Simple tasks, such as operating customer services from a call centre, for example, are inimical to the methods of teamworking. However, for most organizations the evidence is clear: not only do teams work, but they also bring benefits to all.

WORK SOLUTION 1

A task for a team?

So, should you introduce teams or not? Painting a supertanker's hull requires a group of painters, working in parallel on their own particular sections; thus teamworking offers no advantage. On the other hand, a lifeboat crew would need to work in a team, sharing some skills and combining specializations (one might be a brilliant pilot, another might have paramedical skills, and so on). Do the following exercise to assess the breadth of the task. If your responses are predominantly "yes", the job would benefit from teamwork.

1. Is the task a complete process or piece of work, with a start and a finish? Ideal team tasks comprise an entire process or piece of work. Conducting a market research survey for a particular product would qualify, but simply analyzing the statistics would not.

2. Is the brief clear? Ideal team tasks have a clearly defined goal. For example, designing a campaign to launch a new product would be a clear-cut task for an advertising team. By contrast, the multitude of ongoing administrative tasks that arise in all organizations are better tackled by secretaries working in parallel.

3. Is the task challenging? Teams are well-suited to complex tasks that are beyond the abilities of an individual – even when provided with an assistant.

4. Is the task multi-faceted? Does it call upon a range of skills that a single individual is unlikely to possess? For example, the task of creating an in-house company magazine requires photographic, design and editorial skills.

5. Does the task require people to work interdependently – communicating, sharing information and debating decisions about the best way to do the job?

TEAM COMPETENCIES

Successful teams tend to display competence in certain key areas. To be an effective team manager you need to understand these competencies and your role in fostering them within your team. You will need to assess your team's strengths on a continual basis, and seek solutions to any shortfalls that emerge from your assessment.

Competent teams are guided by a concise and compelling vision of the team's overall purpose, which all team members understand and buy into. This is underpinned by four or five challenging objectives that summarize the goals of the team in practical, concrete terms (see pp.90–93). Each team member is skillful at setting goals and managing their own performance as well as the performance of the team as a whole. You might find it helpful to think of the analogy of a good sports team where players constantly help by encouraging and gently cajoling their team mates.

A good team is characterized by a general sense of mutual support, safety and trust, with members able to rely on one another in times of difficulty, and to take creative risks knowing they will be backed up by their colleagues. Adopting a supportive role as team manager does much to promote such an atmosphere in your team, as other team members will be inspired by your example to follow suit (see pp.84–7).

A supportive team atmosphere is often one with strong social bonds between members. Such bonds give the team a cohesion that allows it to ride out the bad times, as well as boosting the contentment of team members, improving work performance and commitment to the job (see pp.84-7).

Crucial to team effectiveness is good communication between team members. They should communicate openly and supportively at all times, listening actively and using direct and respectful speech. As in many other areas of team competence, the team manager takes the lead by honing his or her communication skills (see pp.52–7) in order to train the team accordingly.

The most creative teams are generally the most diverse, and it is the job of the team manager to build an eclectic team (see pp.66–9). Where there is diversity of team membership, there is variety of opinion and debate, which often leads to successful and creative problem-solving. The team manager can facilitate this process by steering the focus of the debate and guiding all parties toward innovative solutions that meet the needs of everyone concerned (see pp.100–103). In particular, successful teams debate constructively how to improve the quality of service or product they offer to clients. This commitment to excellence is a key criterion for judging the performance of any team.

The downside of team diversity is a greater potential for damaging interpersonal clashes within the team, or disagreements as to who should do which task. As team manager it is your responsibility to distinguish between constructive and destructive conflicts, fostering the former and discouraging the latter (see pp.104–107). However, all team members should in fact be able to make this distinction.

Regular team meetings present opportunities to play out and resolve such conflicts. They also provide the forum for vital team processes such as information-sharing, planning, negotiating workloads, synchronizing activities and decision-making of various kinds. As team manager you can facilitate these processes by encouraging everyone to participate in discussions, and preventing domination by single individuals (see pp.96–9). This ensures that all team members have a personal stake in decisions that are taken and plans that are laid. In competent teams many of the decisions are made collectively under the guidance of the team manager. Of course, not every decision is a collective one – an army officer does not conduct a team brainstorming session when the platoon is attacked!

As part of their schedule of meetings, successful teams regularly take time out to review the progress and performance of the team and of individual members. By reflecting on objectives and team processes, teams can keep track of goals that have not been met, pinpoint the reasons for any delays or other problems, and take action to remedy the situation. Such action depends on feedback mechanisms that enable the team to self-correct. As a team manager, you need to initiate this self-reflexive process, providing a model of constructive feedback that the team can follow to regulate their own performance (see pp.112–15).

WORK SOLUTION 2

Assessing the competencies of your team

Perhaps the most accurate way to assess the competencies of your team is to gather feedback from team members on their experiences of working in the team. Ask each member to fill in a copy of this questionnaire and return it to you. Use this information, together with your own responses, to identify those areas where team competencies can be improved (indicated by the statements marked "no"). It is in these areas that you should target your interventions, using the tools presented later in the book.

Please respond to the following statements by ticking the relevant box: Yes No

The team has a clear and compelling vision. ☐ ☐

The team has four or five challenging objectives. ☐ ☐

I am clear about my individual role and personal goals. ☐ ☐

I understand how my role and goals relate to the team vision. ☐ ☐

I feel safe and supported in the team environment. ☐ ☐

I have forged close relationships with my fellow team members. ☐ ☐

Communication within the team is generally clear, direct

and respectful. ☐ ☐

The team comprises a diverse cross-section of individuals. ☐ ☐

Differences of opinion are respected within the team. ☐ ☐

Conflict is generally constructive, leading to creative win–win

solutions. ☐ ☐

Team meetings take place regularly. ☐ ☐

Everyone participates in team processes; no one dominates. ☐ ☐

Regular reviews take place to assess performance and progress. ☐ ☐

The team uses constructive feedback to regulate its performance. ☐ ☐

The team uses constructive feedback to regulate individual

performance. ☐ ☐

TYPES OF TEAMS

Organizations can host many different types of teams, each of which requires a slightly different management approach.

Production and service teams include assembly teams, maintenance, mining and construction teams, accounts teams, sales teams and health-care teams. Such groupings form the main team for most of their members. They have a long life-span, providing an ongoing product or service to clients, customers or the organization. Consequently their objectives and course of action are generally clear. When managing such teams, adopt a long-term strategy focusing on regular appraisals and reviews (see pp.112–15) and ongoing skill development (see pp.144–5). This will promote a drive for improvement and innovation, while ensuring team members feel continually challenged and motivated in their work.

Project and development teams include research teams and product development teams. Dedicated to a particular project, such teams have limited lifespans and a clear set of short-term objectives geared toward performing the task as efficiently as possible. Much of the manager's role entails planning and monitoring progress (see pp.108–111). However, because such teams are short-lived, there is little opportunity for team building. As a result, communication often suffers and conflicts are common, sometimes leading to loss of cohesion within the team. To combat this problem, coach the team in effective communication (see pp.80–83) and where necessary deploy conflict-resolution skills (see pp.126-7).

Advice and involvement teams, such as working parties (teams dedicated to improving working conditions or practices within a company), quality circles (teams that meet with a view to improving the products or services offered by an organization) and staff-involvement groups (which meet to represent staff views to top management), tend to have a short lifespan and are often not the main team for their members. Skills development is not a priority. Instead ensure that the team develops clear and time-limited objectives as well as a concrete plan for implementation (see pp.108–9). Once the team has achieved these objectives, disband the team quickly: too many committees meet long after they need to because they lack clear objectives.

Crews, such as airline crews and electrical-repair teams, are often formed quickly from members who have rarely or never worked together before. Everyone must have a clear understanding of their roles on arrival. Despite flight-deck crew training sessions, most airline accidents occur during the first leg of duty when pilot and co-pilot are working together for the first time. Such teams need clear directives to ensure they operate by the book with maximum efficiency.

Action and negotiation teams, such as surgical and legal teams, comprise members who tend to work together regularly. They have well-developed processes and clear objectives. As manager, pay particular attention to planning processes, ensuring that strategies are prepared for every eventuality (see pp.108–111). Organize reviews after each action period to enable the team to learn from any mistakes (see pp.112–15).

TEAM MANAGEMENT STYLES

There are two main styles of team management: a transactional, task-oriented approach and a transformational, people-oriented approach. Although both styles have similar goals (to complete the task and ensure a high level of performance), they employ different methods to achieve them.

Managers who take a transactional approach to managing their teams concentrate their efforts on finding practical ways to improve team processes. In this context, they view the behaviour of team members as an extension of team processes, and they attempt to modify that behaviour through punishments and rewards. These often take the form of more interesting and challenging projects for those who perform well, and less attractive ones for those who fail to match expectations. The key to using a transactional style successfully lies in rewarding and punishing transparently, ensuring a fair balance of work and setting up a system for monitoring the group's ongoing efforts. Team members must feel that the process is open, just, and free of prejudices.

By contrast, managers who apply a transformational approach pay more attention to team members than to processes, seeking to transform members' images of themselves in relation to the work and the team as a whole. To do this, transformational managers are often charismatic leading lights. They exemplify optimism, a positive approach and team spirit, encouraging members to adopt a similar attitude and inspiring them to action with compelling visions of their future. Transformational managers also provide support and coaching for individual team members, helping them to

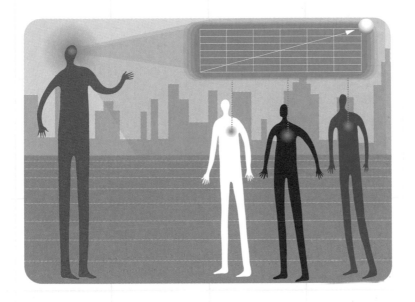

resolve difficulties as well as working to develop their knowledge, skills, abilities and careers.

It is my experience that the most effective managers use
a combination of both of these management styles in their
efforts to improve team performance, shifting their approach
according to the situation that prevails. However, there is a
tendency for some managers to emphasize the transactional
approach – largely because it is easier to make concrete,
measurable improvements to the mechanics of teamworking
than it is to get involved in "fuzzy" people issues. Yet teams
are all about people – by definition they concern individuals
interacting, working and innovating together – so it is vital
that, as team manager, you are able to work confidently within both these styles and are attuned to the requirements of
any given situation (see pp.28–31).

THE ESSENCE OF TEAM MANAGEMENT

The ideal team manager is one who shifts seamlessly between transactional and transformational styles, depending on the situation. It is helpful, therefore, to develop a holistic picture of team management that combines the key elements of both styles into a single model. This allows us to define the role of the team manager in terms of three aspects – managing, leading and coaching. The tasks of managing are those usually associated with a transactional style; the tasks of leading and coaching are those associated with a transformational style.

The *managing* aspect of your role relates to the mechanics of setting up and running a team. As manager you are responsible for building a balanced team, establishing and distributing individual team roles, ensuring that workloads are fair and balanced, and that team members understand

THE LESSONS OF SPORTS TEAMS

For thousands of years team games have allowed us to practise the teamwork so essential to our survival. What do they teach us?

Create early wins. Teams that get ahead first in the game are more likely to win. Make the earliest tasks in a team's life easy to achieve.

Find time to practise. Take time out from pressured work to experiment with new ways of working as a team.

Have a half-time. Half-way through a team project, assess the work completed so far and take time to review and develop new strategies.

Keep the team intact. The longer the same members play together, the better they will become at playing together.

Study the video after the game. At the end of a project or task, ask "What did we do well?" and "What did we do poorly?" Use the responses to improve your team's performance in the future.

their responsibilities and boundaries of power. You are in charge of setting clear, concrete and measurable objectives and ensuring that these are met. Once the team is up and running, it is your role to organize, plan and facilitate team meetings and processes, in addition to implementing a system of rewards and incentives to influence people's actions where appropriate. Performing these tasks demands time-management skills and excellent organizational and planning abilities, as well as clarity, focus and assertiveness.

In order to *lead* your team successfully, you need to provide a role model, setting an example of the kind of actions and values that you wish members to demonstrate. As leader you are also responsible for shaping and communicating an inspiring vision that will motivate the team. If there is a crisis or deadlock, you may be called upon to take charge of the situation. It is also your role to represent the team at a higher level, mediating between the team and the organization. To fulfill these tasks requires honesty, integrity and the courage to act, as well as a certain charisma and social awareness.

The *coaching* aspect of team management requires you to play a more supportive, pastoral role. At the beginning of the team's life, this may involve facilitating some of the difficult transitions in the early stages of team formation, and establishing a warm and nurturing team atmosphere. As the team evolves, you are responsible for helping members to manage their professional relationships, improving their communication and mediating in any disputes. It is your place to monitor their learning, coaching them through the processes of the team, enabling them to acquire new skills, and conducting ongoing appraisals and reviews. To do so you need to develop your own communication and empathy skills in order to respond in an appropriate way to team members.

Weaving together the different strands of your role is a challenging task. Whether you are playing the manager, leader or coach will depend on the particular demands of each moment. To move with ease between the three requires a certain amount of confidence, flexibility and sensitivity. These are qualities that develop over time, nurtured by self-awareness and a willingness to make mistakes, listen to feedback and adapt your approach accordingly. In the next chapter we look at ways in which you can develop these competencies. To transform your team you must first transform yourself.

TEAM MANAGEMENT QUESTIONNAIRE

Ask your team members to rate your management competence using this questionnaire. For the purposes of scoring, 1 = not at all; 2 = a little; 3 = a moderate amount; 4 = quite a lot; 5 = a great deal. If you score less than an average of 4 per section, you can hone your team-management skills by following the advice given in this book.

To what extent does the team manager ...   1 2 3 4 5

MANAGE
- *Clarify what results are expected from the team's work.* ☐☐☐☐☐
- *Help the team to organize and coordinate their work activities to avoid delays, duplication of effort and wasted resources.* ☐☐☐☐☐
- *Ensure that all team members contribute their knowledge and expertise to team decisions.* ☐☐☐☐☐
- *Check the team's work progress against plans to see if it is on target.* ☐☐☐☐☐
- *Regularly check the quality of the team's work.* ☐☐☐☐☐
- *Recognize good performance or extra effort made by team members.* ☐☐☐☐☐

LEAD
- *Communicate a compelling team vision.* ☐☐☐☐☐
- *Encourage the team to look at problems from a different perspective.* ☐☐☐☐☐
- *Encourage collaboration with other teams.* ☐☐☐☐☐
- *Help the team to acquire the resources it needs to conduct its work.* ☐☐☐☐☐

COACH
- *Make themselves available to team members to discuss a problem or particular issue.* ☐☐☐☐☐
- *Treat each team member as an individual with different needs, abilities and aspirations.* ☐☐☐☐☐
- *Provide encouragement and support when the team has a difficult or stressful task.* ☐☐☐☐☐
- *Give helpful feedback to the team and assist them in developing a plan for improvement.* ☐☐☐☐☐

chapter 2

SELF-MANAGEMENT

As team manager you are the most visible and powerful member of the team. Consequently, team members are likely to look to you for a model of how to behave. It is therefore essential that you are able to manage yourself effectively, demonstrating the skills that you wish to cultivate in them.

In this chapter we explore each of these skills, looking at why they are important and how you can develop them within yourself. We begin on a practical level by examining how you can use your time more effectively for the benefit of team members. Next we proceed to a more personal level by exploring self-awareness, which enables us to monitor our thoughts, feelings and actions on a moment-by-moment basis. Using this information, together with feedback from others, you can take steps toward improving the quality and effectiveness of your interactions with the team. These involve managing your thoughts and emotions to create a positive team climate, dealing assertively with conflict, building resonance between members, improving communication and accruing power within the organization.

TIME MANAGEMENT

The role of team manager is extremely diverse, involving concrete, practical tasks as well as less tangible, interpersonal ones. You are likely to face a barrage of demands from team members as well as others in the organization. With so many claims on your attention and only a limited amount of time, you will need well-honed time-management skills in order to stay abreast of your work.

This is important both for you and your team. With your workload under control, you will feel less stressed at work, have more leisure time and experience a greater sense of self-worth and confidence. In turn, when your team members witness you managing your time effectively, they will have greater respect for you and learn by your example. The team as a whole will perform its job with greater ease, thereby reducing stress levels for everyone.

DELEGATE, DUMP OR DEFER?

Delegation, dumping and deferral are three ways of dealing with tasks when under pressure. Delegation involves assigning a task to someone else, but retaining responsibility for ensuring that it is done to an appropriate standard. Dumping involves handing over both the responsibility and the task to someone else. Deferral involves keeping the task for yourself, but putting it off until a later date. All three are valid strategies of task management, but must be used appropriately to be effective. When choosing between the three, consider whether the task really needs doing, and if so, whether it needs to be done by you. If the task is not urgent, you may be able to defer it until a later date. If the task is urgent but doesn't require your personal attention, you can delegate or dump, provided that there is sufficient time to communicate the requirements of the task to the team member concerned. When dumping ensure the team member has sufficient skills and authority to take responsibility for the task; when delegating be prepared to offer support where necessary. In both cases guard against piling more work upon already overloaded team members.

The basic principle of time management involves focusing your efforts in the areas where you can provide most benefit. Bear in mind the 80–20 rule, reflecting the likelihood that 80 per cent of your efforts will focus on doing 20 per cent of the work. To decide which activities constitute the 20 per cent that really makes a difference to your performance, you need to distinguish between the tasks that are important and those that are urgent. All too often, we work from moment to moment, doing the next most urgent task – with the result that we neglect important aspects of our role.

Overcoming this tendency requires self-discipline and a longer-term perspective. The first step is to spend ten minutes each morning identifying the 20 per cent – your top four or five priorities for the day. These might include analyzing customer feedback in preparation for an important call to a supplier, designing a presentation, or drawing up an agenda for the next team meeting. A particular priority for you as team manager should be managing the people on your team – talking to them, tracking their work, checking their welfare and offering coaching and support where necessary.

Once you have identified your priorities, make a list of all the tasks that you are facing. Then, on the basis of your priorities, assign a weighting of importance to them on a scale from one to five, with one being least important and five being most important. From this you will be able to gauge which tasks require your attention first. For a longer-term perspective, conduct this process on a monthly and yearly basis, taking an hour at the beginning of each month and a day at the beginning of each year to prioritize your tasks.

Having established how you *should* be using your time, you may find it helpful to analyze how you *are* currently using your time. A comparison of the two will then give you a clearer sense of the most effective way to redistribute your energies. One way to do this is to keep a journal of your working activities for a week, indicating how much time you are spending on different tasks and the extent to which those tasks are important (see Work Solution 3, opposite).

As well as engaging in these processes yourself, encourage team members to pursue similar strategies of time management. Provide clear direction by continually emphasizing the priorities of the team. This will help team members to prioritize their work, boosting not only the efficacy, but also the happiness and wellbeing of the team as a whole.

WORK SOLUTION 3

Keeping a time-management journal

In order to use your time more effectively, it is important to understand how you are currently distributing your time. One way to do this is to keep a special time-management journal for five days. This exercise leads you through the process and shows you how to interpret and utilize the findings.

1. In a notebook allocate one page to each day of the working week. Divide each of the five pages into two sections – one for the morning and one for the afternoon. If you prefer, set up a spreadsheet on the computer to perform the same function, or use a pre-formatted paper journal.

2. Start the journal on a Monday. At lunchtime, take a break to list the tasks that you have been working on during the morning, noting how much time you spent on each task, and how important the task was in relation to your priorities on a scale of one (least important) to five (most important). Repeat this process at the end of the afternoon. Follow this pattern for the rest of the week.

3. At the end of the week, list all of the tasks that you have done in rank order of importance from one to five. Beside each one note down the total time spent on the task during the course of the week. Use this information to analyze the distribution of your time, working out which tasks are receiving too much time and which ones too little on the basis of their importance.

4. Set objectives and a concrete action plan detailing changes you can make to your working practices that will help you to allocate your time more effectively. To help you do this, ask for suggestions from a mentor or from another team manager whose work you admire. Finally, implement your plan.

SELF-AWARENESS

Research indicates that teams develop a shared emotional climate. This evolves out of members' interactions with one another and tends to be self-reinforcing, creating either virtuous circles of optimism, enthusiasm and excitement, or vicious circles of anxiety, hostility and depression. The nature of the emotional climate has a significant impact on the success of the team: a positive climate boosts members' productivity and effectiveness; a negative climate breeds absenteeism and poor performance.

The conduct of team managers has a particularly powerful effect on the emotional climates of their teams. This is because they provide role models for other team members.

For this reason it is vital for you to monitor the effect you are having on your team. This requires self-awareness – a skill that enables us to keep tabs on our thoughts, feelings and actions on a moment-by-moment basis. This is much easier to do when we are by ourselves in a quiet place – on a deserted beach gazing quietly out to sea, for example. However, with practice, you will be able to keep the spotlight of self-awareness switched on at all times.

In the longer term, self-awareness creates a stronger sense of self – an understanding of not only our strengths and weaknesses, but also our guiding values, the intangibles that are important to us. Such inner coherence is an important leadership quality: if your conduct is consistent with your values, you will become an independent and decisive thinker, unswayed by outside pressures and able to make the right choices for both yourself and your team. Perceiving these signs of strength and integrity, your team is, in turn, more likely to trust and follow you.

So how can we develop greater self-awareness? An important first step is to take time out once a day for 15 to 20 minutes of solitary reflection. You could take a quiet walk alone in the stillness of the early morning or close your office door and block phone-calls during your lunchbreak. Use this period alone to acknowledge and reflect on your current state of being – your feelings, thoughts and behaviour. Consider too whether there is anything here you would change, and if so what you can do to achieve this.

To conduct a more concrete appraisal of yourself, note your moods at regular intervals during the day. If you find this difficult to remember, post a reminder onto your computer or set a watch or timer to go off every hour or so. Your notes need not involve long, involved descriptions of your experiences, they can be as simple as single words or colour-coded symbols, denoting particular behaviours or feelings, together with the accompanying circumstances or events. For example, "4pm: Irritated and frustrated after long, unproductive meeting with HR director." If you read through these notes at the end of each week, you may discern patterns in the flow of your responses, and gain a greater awareness of your emotional triggers. You can use this information to avert similar situations in the future. You might conclude, for example, that next time you need information from the HR director, you will email a request instead of arranging a meeting, or you will go to the meeting armed with a clear agenda and aim to keep the encounter short and productive.

In this way, you will find that gradually you develop a constant awareness of all that is here and now in your experience. As well as noticing your own thoughts, feelings and conduct, you will develop a heightened sensitivity to those of the people around you, thereby enhancing your ability to relate to and manage your team.

As you become more aware of your shortcomings and limitations, it is essential to adopt an attitude of compassion toward yourself. For example, you may notice a tendency to vent your feelings of irritation and frustration on others. If you respond to such limitations by beating yourself up and feeling guilty, you will not only engender a spiral of negativity, but you will also find yourself hiding your weaknesses, thereby limiting your capacity for self-awareness. Conversely, if you view your limitations with compassion, they become opportunities for growth and development. Once you extend this attitude toward yourself, you will also develop greater compassion toward others, enabling you to forge stronger relationships with your team.

WORK SOLUTION 4

Meditating into mindfulness

Meditation is the art of paying attention. It is an excellent method for developing self-awareness; as scientific research has demonstrated, it also boosts creativity, increases positive emotion and aids relaxation. This exercise provides a simple introduction to the practice of meditation. Perform it once or twice a day for ten minutes when you have a quiet moment to yourself – ideally early in the morning and before your evening meal. Approach the exercise with an open, contented heart and frame of mind.

1. Find a quiet place and sit upright but comfortably, either on a floor cushion or on an upright chair.

2. Close your eyes and enjoy the stillness of simply sitting for a few moments.

3. Focus your attention on one of the physical sensations of your breathing – perhaps the sensation of the breath as it enters and leaves your nostrils, or the gentle movements of your belly and chest, whichever feels most comfortable.

4. Retaining your focus on an aspect of your breathing, say the word "one" silently to yourself, each time you breathe out. If you find that your focus is distracted by external noises or intrusive thoughts, simply treat these interruptions as clouds drifting across the sky of your mind – do not try to push them away and do not hold on to them, just allow them to pass through your consciousness. Then, when you are ready, return your attention to the physical sensation of your breath and the repetition of the word "one".

5. Continue this exercise for ten minutes, or for as long as feels comfortable. Then slowly open your eyes and sit quietly for a few moments, before getting up.

RECEIVING FEEDBACK

We gain awareness of ourselves not only through introspection, but also by listening to the feedback that we receive from others in the form of compliments, criticism and more subtle non-verbal responses. People give us feedback all the time, but all too often we tend to disbelieve it, ignore it or get upset by it rather than take it in and act upon it. The trick is to regard all feedback as a useful source of information about our impact on others, which we can act upon if we choose.

As team manager your most important source of feedback is your team. As well as paying close attention to how team members respond to you on a daily basis, be prepared to ask them direct questions, such as "Am I being clear about the direction of the work?" and "Am I supporting you enough?" If you are to continue to obtain honest feedback it is critical that you respond appropriately to their replies. Whether positive or negative, receive all feedback graciously and ensure that you have fully understood its import by summarizing your understanding of the message. Then take time to consider the feedback using judicious discrimination. If members' comments seem valid, you can seek to adjust your actions accordingly, reinforcing the positive and working to counter the negative.

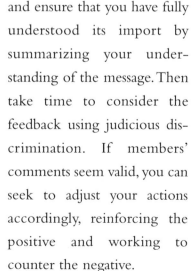

WORK SOLUTION 5

Dealing with formal feedback

**Supplement daily feedback from your team with information gathered on a
more formal basis – once a year if your team is ongoing, or more frequently
if your team has a shorter lifespan. This exercise takes you through the
process of gathering, collating and evaluating formal feedback.**

1. Gather feedback formally from team members by distributing questionnaires
(see p.31) to all team members and asking them to complete them anonymously
and return them to you. If you have a well-established relationship with your
team, you may be able to do this in an open forum with all members present,
calling on each in turn to give you feedback on your strengths and weaknesses
in the main areas of managing, leading and coaching.

2. Collate the responses of team members by grouping the information, whether
positive or negative, according to the managing, leading and coaching skill-sets.
Evaluate the feedback for each skill-set in turn. Identify common themes and
information that rings true – these points are likely to be the most valid. Look
critically at contradictions and anomalies to assess their usefulness. Summarize
all valid and useful information as a series of points for each skill-set.

3. Arrange a meeting with team members to discuss the findings. If certain
points require clarification, request additional feedback. Ask for suggestions of
ways to improve your functioning as a team manager. On the basis of these,
create a series of action points with accompanying objectives.

4. Work toward your objectives by implementing the action points. Review the
effect of these changes on team effectiveness, say, once every two months.

DEALING WITH NEGATIVE EMOTIONS

Evidence suggests that when negative emotions become chronic, they can have a damaging effect on mental and physical health. As we have seen, the mood of the team manager has a powerful impact on the team's emotional climate, which in turn affects the productivity of the team (see p.38). It is therefore important for you to deal effectively with your negative emotions, for your own sake and that of the team.

Frustration is a negative emotion, which is commonly experienced in the workplace and occurs when our needs are blocked. If you experience frustration, try to distance yourself from your feelings in order to identify the needs that are not being met. Then analyze the blockages to those needs – for example, the conflicting need of another person. Once you have a clearer understanding of the situation, you are in a better position to find a creative solution to the problem.

Similar to frustration is anger, an emotion that usually erupts when we feel slighted or abused. When you feel angry

COPING WITH PANIC

When anxiety gets out of hand it can spiral into panic. Whenever this occurs we feel like we are losing control – a terrifying experience that leaves us feeling completely helpless. If panic threatens to overwhelm you, the most important thing is to recognize that the panic will pass. The recommendation of many self-help groups is to repeat, almost mantra-like, the phrase: "This too will pass, this too will pass." Another effective strategy is to focus attention on breathing slowly and deeply, counting the breaths until the anxiety subsides.

If you know in advance that you will encounter a difficult situation, take time to prepare yourself beforehand. This will increase your sense of control and help to ward off any panic before it arises.

with anyone it is vital not to lose your temper. Shouting is the surest way to destroy team morale. If the emotion threatens to overwhelm you, take some time out from the situation and try to unwind. Once you have calmed down, analyze the reasons why you felt so upset, and come up with an objective solution to the problem. Then return to the situation and seek to apply that solution as dispassionately and effectively as possible.

Another common negative emotion is anxiety. Most forms of anxiety are caused by fear of loss. For example, if we are giving a presentation, we may be afraid of making an error and losing our reputation. One way to cope with such anxiety is to use it as a source of positive energy: in this instance, expressing it through confident, expressive speech and vigorous hand gestures that enliven the presentation.

POSITIVE THINKING

It is vital to be aware of our thoughts as well as our emotions. This is because how we think has a considerable impact on how we feel. If we think optimistic thoughts, we are more likely to feel positive, and vice versa. As we have more control over how we think than how we feel, we can do much to create an upbeat team atmosphere by thinking positively.

The first step to positive thinking is recognizing when you have negative thoughts (see pp.38–41). Whenever you catch yourself moaning or catastrophizing, whether inwardly or outwardly, try to change your mental cassette tape for one that focuses on being positive, effective and supportive. At the same time, identify the underlying reason for any negative thoughts. If there is something you can do to resolve the problem, take action rather than complaining helplessly about it. For example, if you are grumbling because a team member has not performed some work to an acceptable standard, speak to the individual concerned in order to address the issue. If there seems to be no obvious cause for your negative thought patterns, it may be that you are tired or overworked. If so, give yourself a break and recharge your batteries. You'll think and feel more positive as a result.

If the cause of the problem lies beyond your control, there are several ways to approach the situation more positively. The first involves reframing events in a positive light. For example, if you find yourself in conflict with another department, view the situation as an opportunity for finding a creative solution that satisfies the needs of both parties. A similar strategy involves rationalizing setbacks positively. For example, if you fail to recruit a new team member because they go to another organization, you can see this as an opportunity to save resources in the short-term while you look for an even better candidate to fill the vacancy.

Another option is to harness the power of the self-fulfilling prophecy. As the psychologist Albert Bandura has demonstrated, the beliefs we hold about our abilities have a powerful effect on our performance. If we set up positive expectations about our success in a situation, we are likely to tackle the situation in a positive way and expect others to view us positively, which in turn inspires them to do so. This increases the likelihood of our success, reinforcing our self-belief and making similar scenarios more likely to occur in the future.

LAUGHTER IN THE WORKPLACE

Laughter communicates that we pose no threat. It is a signal to those around us that we are relaxed, friendly and unguarded. In the workplace laughter is therefore a positive sign of trust and ease among team members. It builds a sense of community as well as easing tension and stimulating creative thinking. As neuroscientists have demonstrated, laughter is highly contagious, so you can encourage it within your team by laughing readily yourself. It is not necessary to be a great wit to bring laughter to your team – most laughter occurs not in response to sophisticated jokes, but as a result of light remarks that seem mundane in the recounting. Use laughter to defuse the tension of awkward moments and look for the funny side of difficult situations. Remember to be sensitive to the needs of others. Humour becomes negative when teasing is uncomfortable for its target. You should encourage team members to confront humour that is offensive, harrassing or bullying and to report it to you when it is sustained.

BEING ASSERTIVE

As a team manager you are bound to experience difficulties from time to time with someone in your team. You can be passive, which means doing nothing and pretending that the problem doesn't exist. You can be passively aggressive, which means that you avoid contact and take steps to undermine them. Or you can be aggressive. All these responses are unconstructive and inappropriate for a team manager.

By contrast, assertiveness is the natural and reasonable response of a manager, who is engaging in a difficult exchange with a potentially uncompromising employee. To be assertive is to make clear to the person responsible what your true reactions are to their behaviour and what you expect to happen. It is usually important to be clear about the consequences of what they have done or said, especially when negligence or thoughtlessness is involved: otherwise your remarks may seem unjust.

Do not shy away from the use of the first person, "I", when expressing your reactions, but do make every effort to control any underlying emotions (see pp.44–5). Speak clearly and confidently, and try not to give the impression that you are uncertain what to say, or that you are hesitantly softening your message out of consideration for the other's feelings. If you encounter disagreement, use the "broken record" technique, whereby you repeat your points in different words, rather than allow yourself to be distracted from the essence of your argument. Concentrate on reaching agreement with the team member about their future conduct – and get them to make a commitment to the necessary change.

WORK SOLUTION 6

Dealing with difficult team members

Dealing with conflict is rarely easy so it's little wonder that many of us shy away from it when we can. However, as team manager you have a responsibility to confront conflict in a constructive manner by adopting an assertive approach. This exercise will help you to deal with such a confrontation.

1. Beforehand consider the nature of the planned confrontation in terms of your feelings, your needs and your desired outcome. For example, someone in your team is making cynical comments repeatedly during team meetings. This is undermining your authority, making you feel uncomfortable and threatening the team's commitment. Acting assertively, your aim is to persuade that person to change their conduct by telling them of the impact they are having on you and the team and straightforwardly asking them to desist in the future.

2. Rehearse what you are going to say to the person when you confront them. Go through your key points, bearing in mind that the aim is to outline the situation from your perspective, giving concrete examples of recent incidents. Be absolutely clear about what you want. Envisage how you might resolve the conflict in a way that is agreeable to both sides.

3. Choose your time and place carefully. Usually you will want to have the conversation in private, so make sure that you're unlikely to be interrupted.

4. When you address the person, speak in a clear and respectful manner. Work toward the desired commitment to change. Once you achieve this, thank the other person for their time and cooperation. If necessary, agree to meet again to give them the opportunity to think about what you have said.

EMPATHY AND RESONANCE

Empathy is the ability to read, be sensitive to and understand other people's emotions. It is a form of social awareness that develops out of self-awareness (see pp.38–41), for when we learn to recognize and understand our own emotions, we become more conscious of other people's. As a team manager it is essential that you develop the skill of empathy because it enables you to attune your responses to the feelings of individual team members and the group as a whole. In doing so, you will gradually create an atmosphere in which every-one empathizes with everyone else. This process of collective attunement is called *resonance* and is a prerequisite for a supportive and cooperative team climate.

The simplest way to develop empathy is to put yourself in the position of the other person or people by asking yourself "How would I feel in their situation?" Spend time getting to know individual team members. Ask open questions to discover more about their experiences, and ask further questions to establish that you have understood correctly. Explore others' ideas, beliefs and aspirations to discover what motivates them. This information will be of great help when you are trying to establish a common focus for the team (see pp.74–7), as well as when you are helping individual members to improve their skills and develop their careers (see pp.144–5).

Use this opportunity to learn more about the emotional reality of the team by questioning members about their experiences of working within the group. In doing so, be open about your own thoughts and feelings, as this will encourage the others to talk honestly. If you suspect there may be hidden frustrations, probe them gently and supportively. Revealing problems is the first step to resolving them.

Whether the emotions you detect are positive or negative, the important thing is to acknow-ledge them and give people the opportunity to express them. This does not mean exploring every nuance of each member's emotional life, but rather paying attention to those emotions that are having a significant impact – whether on an individual or the team as a whole. For example, if you sense that a team member is feeling frustrated about some-thing, prompt them to express their feelings, either in the context of a team meeting, or alone with you. Just knowing that the team manager is taking their frustrations seriously, with a view to suitable action, will usually go some way toward soothing the employee's agitated mind.

Once you attune yourself to the collective and individual feelings of team members, you can respond sensitively to their needs in a way that moves the group toward greater resonance. Your response could involve calming fears, moder-ating anger, encouraging enthusiasm or identifying with optimism. Offer acknowledgment, understanding and, where appropriate, practical support. By modelling this approach yourself, you set a norm within the team, increasing emo-tional awareness all round.

COMMUNICATION SKILLS

Communication is the foundation of all our relationships. It involves the mutual exchange of information and is therefore central to team functioning, which relies upon the interdependence and cooperation of team members. The most direct forms of communication are active listening, speaking and non-verbal communication. Part of your role is to facilitate relationships within the team, so it is vital that your skills in these areas are excellent, setting the standard for the group.

Active listening

Of all communication skills, listening is probably the most important. This is because our ability to listen determines whether or not we learn anything from an interaction and, therefore, whether actual communication takes place. Listening is an active rather than a passive process, requiring your full attention. Not only do you need to hear what the speaker is saying, but you also need to monitor your response. Next time you are listening to one of your team members speak, ask yourself, "Am I paying attention?" If you find that your mind has drifted away, or you are busy formulating a reply, you will miss the crux of the message. Next ask yourself, "Am I listening with an open mind?" When you listen openly, you suspend judgment until the speaker has fully explained themselves. Try to adopt a neutral attitude rather than leaping to conclusions or engaging in a mental debate about what the other person is saying. This will ensure that your preconceptions about the speaker and the topic do not distort the message you receive.

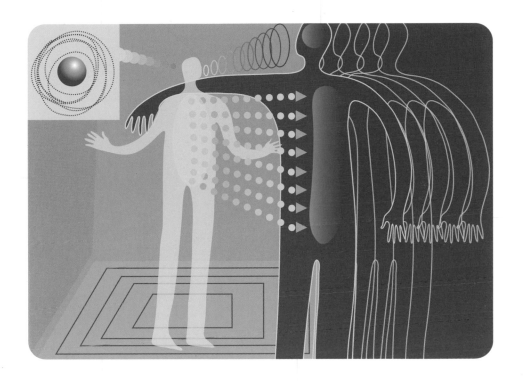

However, it is not enough to listen actively: you also need to demonstrate that you are doing so. This encourages openness in the speaker and increases the likelihood that you will obtain all the information you require. You can show that you are listening actively by smiling, nodding and keeping eye contact. In contrast, fidgeting, interrupting and avoiding eye contact demonstrate that you are not giving the speaker your full attention. Such tendencies are likely to offend the other person and inhibit your understanding of the message.

If aspects of what you are hearing remain unclear, encourage the speaker to expand further, until a mental picture has formed in your head. As a team manager you will often have seen how some people find it difficult to describe events in a chronological order. Be patient with such people, and afterwards go through the sequence again to make sure that you have understood it. If a speaker assumes you know more than you do, admit your unfamiliarity with the topic and ask them to elaborate. Such openness will usually be interpreted as a sign of competence and confidence by team members, who may now feel that they have permission themselves to reveal uncertainty – thus establishing a norm of honest and effective communication within the team.

At every stage during this process, ensure that you have accurately understood the speaker's messages by listening reflectively. This involves summarizing what the speaker has said and asking them to corroborate your understanding. By practising this technique in all your interactions, you will communicate your genuine desire to understand. This will improve all your relationships, both professional and personal.

Speaking

The primary purpose of speech is to convey a message to another person or group of people. To do this effectively you need to think about what you are saying and how you are saying it. Before speaking, make sure that you have your listeners' attention, then speak clearly and succinctly, avoiding rambling digressions and technical jargon. Endeavour to make eye contact with your listener so that you engage them in what you are saying. If there is more than one listener, look at each one in turn so that all feel included. Be as honest as

WORK SOLUTION 7

Preparing a spoken presentation

When speaking in a formal context it is vital to prepare yourself beforehand so that you can communicate the information clearly, logically and coherently. This exercise guides you through the process of preparing a spoken presentation. You can also apply many of the points to other situations requiring preparation, such as a tricky discussion with a team member.

1. Formulate your approach by considering the nature of your audience and the pitch of your speech. What prior knowledge can you assume? How challenging can the concepts be? What information will be most valuable to your audience? How can you convey your message in a way that they will readily understand?

2. To establish the content of your speech, list the key points that you wish to make. Remember audiences are unlikely to absorb more than six key points. Bearing in mind your answers in step 1, plan what you want to say for each key point, writing out the main pieces of information in full. Prepare any visual aids that you will need, such as slides and videos. Keep diagrams as simple and graphic as possible. Avoid endless lists of bullet points.

3. Time the duration of each section to check whether you are spending too long on any one element. Adjust the lengths where necessary. Practise the speech, with your notes in front of you and then unaided, until you have memorized the main points of the content. In addition, rehearse the speech mentally by imagining yourself delivering the presentation perfectly to prime you for success.

4. On the day of your presentation, arrive at the venue in plenty of time in order to check out the room and ensure that your electronic aids are working correctly.

possible to ensure complete understanding. It is helpful to speak slowly, allowing yourself pauses to formulate what you wish to say, rather than rushing blindly into a spate of ad libs.

We may sometimes feel a temptation to bluff when we are uncertain of the facts, employ self-inflated rhetoric when we feel that our arguments are flawed, or even make derisive comments about others when we feel we are under attack. All these are essentially improvised ways to boost our own position. Such tactics can be very damaging to communication, as we are liable to leave out information, waste time or risk hurting other people. To avoid this, always ask yourself, "Is what I wish to say helpful, relevant or important to the team in this situation?"

DECODING NON-VERBAL SIGNS

Non-verbal sign:	Possible meaning:
Occasional laughter	Warmth, engagement, openness
Constant laughter	Anxiety, request for approval
Smiling	Warmth, openness
Hand over mouth	Doubtfulness, holding back
Slouching	Boredom, lack of interest
Avoiding eye contact	Secrecy, shyness
Continual eye contact	Attempt to dominate
Frowning (absorbed)	Concentration
Frowning with a cold stare	Anger, hostility
Continual fidgeting	Anxiety
Repeated finger-tapping	Frustration, irritation
Body oriented toward you	Openness
Body oriented away from you	Self-protection, hiding information
Arms open	Openness
Arms held out wide	Appeal for trust
Arms crossed	Tension, defiance, self-protection
Touching (by higher status person)	Communication of dominance
Touching (by lower status person)	Desire for affiliation or approval

Non-verbal communication

When we interact with each other, we tend to focus on the verbal content of the exchange. However, a great deal of communication takes place on a non-verbal level via facial expression, body language and vocal inflection. For example, constant fidgeting is usually a sign of anxiety; slouching can indicate boredom (see box, opposite). Paying attention to other people's non-verbal behaviour enables us to listen to what is *not* being said – to perceive some of the thoughts and feelings underlying the main message. This can be particularly helpful when trying to gauge the emotions of team members reluctant to communicate their feelings openly. Of course, it is important not to over-interpret these signals – someone crossing their arms may be cold rather than defiant – but where a cluster of signs indicates a common attitude or emotion, it is worth taking seriously.

We can also monitor our own non-verbal behaviour to gain awareness of our emotional state and the effect this may be having on our listeners. For example, if you find yourself nervously shifting your weight while giving a speech, you can consciously still your body to convey more confidence.

Research indicates that when two people communicate effectively, they unconsciously synchronize their body language as empathy and resonance increase. For example, both may lean toward each other, or tilt their heads to one side. By consciously mirroring the body language of team members, they relax, and then you can relax. And so the empathic connection between you is strengthened.

POWER, INFLUENCE AND NETWORKING

Power and politics are interwoven through any organization. Hidden social networks and power relationships create a complex dynamic that will impact on a team in unexpected and sometimes uncontrollable ways. A successful team manager will understand such interactions, and will also be able to work within them to win organizational support to enable the team to do its work – for example, in the form of rewards, training, resources and information.

Influence is another word for power, and you win it from your position, from your capacity to reward, from the actions you have the authority to make, from your expertise, and from your charisma or personality. To use such influence on behalf of your team, the customers and the wider organization is part of your role as team leader. However, it is unwise to use your influence to try to gain benefits for yourself, as this is easily spotted by others, and usually resented.

Charisma can in itself have its downside: some magnetic personalities have a psychological need to have a profound and widespread impact on others. Such people are often risk-takers of the first magnitude, and can bring about dazzling successes – but also on occasion plunge their followers into spectacular failure. As team manager you may encounter invididuals like this in the upper echelons of your organization – in which case, keep your wits about you and avoid the perils of overzealous discipleship. A healthy level of cooperative independence within the team, with everybody taking responsibility for major decisions, can provide an important counterweight to such a dominant influence.

This is not to say that self-confidence, persuasiveness and a very strong belief in oneself are anything but good qualities, and ones that are highly desirable in team management, especially in situations where leadership is required. To foster self-belief you need to know yourself and value yourself (see pp.38–41). Many people find meditation and yoga useful as ways to develop these qualities. An easy but effective exercise, loosely associated with meditation, is to say aloud to yourself over and over again a statement that affirms a particular aspect of your self-belief, such as: "I am creative, effective, honest, kind, and committed to my work."

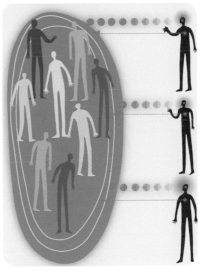

Some may find such approaches too introspective or "New Age" for their tastes, and will prefer to concentrate on building up personal power at a more practical level as their career develops, by acquiring position, experience, maturity, skills (including inter-personal skills) and qualities such as patience and generosity that a team is sure to find praiseworthy.

Of course, there will always be managers within the organization who have more power than you – whether resulting from position or from personal qualities, or a mixture of the two. Unless you can recognize who has the power within an organization and build positive relationships with these people, your team may suffer in its attempts to win resources, which are often the object of competition. Being

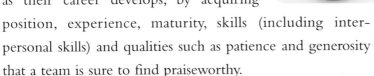

generally pleasant and helpful to people, whatever their status, gains you what is sometimes known as "referent power" – people will do things for you because they like and respect you. And, of course, being pleasant helps to generate a happier, more positive workplace community.

If you have the opportunity to chair important meetings within the organization, take them, as you will then have some control over what is discussed, how it is discussed and how decisions are made.

Often you will be able to improve the effectiveness of your team by building networks, coalitions and alliances – for example, with other teams. Synergies can often be released – all you need is the imagination to see the shared benefits and the communication skills to get everybody else to agree and cooperate. A team that is isolated from everyone else is likely to suffer from missed opportunities of all kinds – as well as possible resource starvation.

Some people associate networking with an endless round of parties and conferences, but in fact the most valuable inter-actions often happen within the workplace as part of the warp and weft of friendly working contact. Ask people how they are and show an interest in their recent experiences: friendly curiosity and concern will not only forge the social bond but also, surprisingly often, yield useful information.

Networking and influence-wielding need not – indeed, must not – be underhand. If you behave openly, honestly and with integrity, you and your team are likely to gain advantages and support within the organization.

WORK SOLUTION 8

The art of persuasion

One strategy for influencing others is to persuade them that what you want them to do, or to agree to, is also in their own best interests. This exercise guides you through the process of preparing and presenting an effective case that operates on this principle.

1. Consider your proposal from the perspective of the person that you hope to persuade. In two columns, list the major advantages and disadvantages of your proposal for the other party. From these lists identify one or two of the most important advantages and one or two of the most important disadvantages, working from the perspective of the other person as much as possible.

2. Work out what changes you can make to your proposal to minimize the disadvantages to the other person. Then work out what changes you can make to your proposal to maximize the advantages.

3. Plan your argument, making a list of bulleted points. Begin with an outline of your proposal. Then acknowledge the potential disadvantages for the other person, explaining how these can be avoided, or at least made more manageable. This will help to reduce the other person's resistance. Finally, outline the advantages of your proposal. Only present your three or four best arguments. If you present ten points in support of your case, people tend to focus on the weakest points not the strongest.

4. Learn the bulleted list by heart and then practise outlining your proposal to the other person in front of the mirror. When you feel quite confident and at ease with your arguments, present your proposal to the other party.

chapter 3

TEAM BUILDING

The principles of team building are relevant to all team managers, whether you are setting up a new team or managing an existing one. Whatever the stage of your team's development, it is never too late to create the conditions for success.

In this chapter we begin by examining the life stages of the team and the changing nature of your role at each stage. Then we look at the process of creating a diverse and balanced team, discussing factors such as gender, cultural background and the skills and experiences necessary for the job. This is followed by general interviewing and recruitment techniques, as well as information about personality models, which together will help you pick the right people for your team.

Having selected team members, the next step is to transform them into a team. To do this we discover how to give members a common sense of identity and values, while clarifying their individual roles. Continuing the theme, we learn ways to improve the communication between team members, and create an atmosphere of support within the team.

STAGES OF TEAM DEVELOPMENT

Teams go through five natural stages of development: forming, storming, norming, performing and adjourning. Your role is busiest during forming and storming. You are less busy during norming and least involved during performing.

At the *forming* stage team members tend to be anxious, asking testing questions: "What is the task? Is it achievable? Will my contribution be fulfilling? What support will you give me?" You must be clear about your role in order to help other people become clear about theirs. Tell them that you will set the overall direction but you expect them to help to define precise objectives; that they should follow an approximate schedule of meetings; and that you will use their expertise in team decision-making. Reassure them that you will learn together, modifying the project plan or long-term brief if necessary as you go along. They will also need to know about resources, budget, IT equipment and admin support, as well as senior managers' expectations of the team, and rulings that will affect working methods (such as the

need for confidentiality). Have all this information ready. Ensure that you can clearly state the overall objective and plan, and make these available in written form.

The *storming* stage occurs after the team has first formed and before roles are clearly worked out. Team members may compete for tasks that seem to offer status or the chance to learn new skills. This is the time for you to encourage debate and discussion about the means to achieve the team's goals. But first make it clear how you see your own role – the kind of support you will be able to give, the extent to which you will rely on team members' skills and experience, and the kind of crisis into which you will step to provide direction. Seek also to establish norms of openness, courtesy and empathy within the team as they work through any conflicts.

In the *norming* phase, which often occurs after about four weeks of weekly meetings, explicit and implicit "norms" are established. Implicit norms might be that team members can arrive late for meetings if they are very busy; that it's good for people to offer supportive comments to each other; or that it's acceptable to blame senior management for certain problems. Such rules are established by members observing what behaviour is accepted. More explicit rules may be agreed by consensus as priorities in a meeting called for the purpose (for example, never be disrespectful to customers). Implicit norms that you feel are undesirable can, of course, be raised in discussion with a view to changing them.

In the longest phase, of *performing*, team members are getting on with the job and succeeding in meeting objectives. Your role becomes more that of coach, available to help members explore, clarify and resolve problems. Establish regular reviews to ensure that the team continues to be effective and responsive to its environment.

CREATING A BALANCED TEAM

Creating a balanced team means ensuring that the people you choose have the skills to get the job done, but also have sufficiently diverse backgrounds to create a powerful group dynamic. Teams of like-minded clones will enjoy a comfortable existence but will be ineffective and creatively stagnant. Diversity in age, skills, culture, and life and work experience ensures a variety of perspectives in team work and decision-making. This will translate into effectiveness and high levels of innovation once you coach team members to see their differences as a valuable asset rather than as a possible threat to their individuality.

As you begin to build your team, your first priority is to find people who have the right balance of skills and experience. Begin by drawing up a list of the skills required to accomplish the team's task. For example, imagine you have been asked to put together a team to create a staff attitude survey for an organization with country-wide outlets (such as gas stations). The task requires someone with experience of questionnaire design; a statistician to help with the questionnaire and analyze the data; someone with experience of setting up a telephone help-desk for staff to call when they have questions in relation to the survey; and a skilled project manager with experience of running surveys across multiple sites. It would also be useful to include someone who can create a website related to the survey.

Once you have drawn up a skills list, you need to select the people who match these requirements. Assessing the skills of potential team members is done in two main ways: first from their résumés; second by interviewing them (see pp.70–71). The more the interview focuses on their experience of using the relevant skills in recent employment, the better. Of course, the interview also gives you an opportunity to learn about the individual's life experi-

ence and personality (see pp.72–3). From shortlisted candidates you can start to select your team, aiming to create a balance of applicable knowledge and diversity of experience. You may decide to favour candidates who have worked together in teams in the past.

A good gender balance in your team will enhance the positive effects of diversity. In our research with more than 1,000 teams, we have found that the more women there are in a team (excluding women-only teams), the better everyone in the team says it functions. Our videos of team meetings reveal that women tend to focus more on the participation and involvement of their colleagues, whereas men are more likely to focus on the task. Teams that combine these two perspectives tend to have a more rounded approach to getting the job done, so that the soft and hard aspects of teamwork are both well-managed.

Try to build multiculturalism into your team if you can. We live in a global village where international travel and communication are the norm. Societies, too, are increasingly multicultural, so teams must mirror the diversity in the communities that they serve if they are to respond knowledgeably to the needs of customers.

If possible, try to ensure over time (for example, through an appropriate rewards and incentive system) that you have a high percentage of long-serving members in your team. The longer teams are together, the better they tend to perform because the participants have a clear understanding of each other's working styles. Of course, new members joining from time to time bring in new perspectives and challenges.

Diversity may bring difficulties as well as benefits. When you bring together a wide range of ages, skills, cultural backgrounds and life experiences, there is a strong possibility of friction. But ideally these differences will be the grit in the oyster that produces the pearl. For this to happen you, as manager, must create the right medium. You must model the skills of teamwork (see Chapter 2) and emphasize the team's shared goals. At the same time, demonstrate that dissent can be valuable by highlighting it – for example, you might say in a team meeting: "I think Naomi sees things differently on this issue. Let's take some time to consider her view and make sure that we are not missing something really important here." When diversity leads to so much argument that the team is no longer functioning effectively (for example, members failing to agree on objectives), give the team responsibility for changing the way it is working. Talk individually to those people who are causing the most difficulties and ask them how you can help them to overcome the conflict.

Generally, the storming and norming phases are longer in diverse teams than they are in homogenous ones, but if you help your members to work with and integrate their different perspectives, you will nurture both effectiveness and innovation. Sparkling fountains take more effort and ingenuity to create, but they are more fun to splash around in than stagnant pools.

THE ART OF EFFECTIVE TEAM BUILDING

One way to encourage the members of diverse teams to work more effectively together is to engage in team-building processes during the course of the team's development, particularly during the storming and norming phases. Often when we think of team building, we imagine specially organized outward-bound activities, such as rock climbing and caving, or group exercises, such as figuring out how to cross a river using plastic barrels, wooden poles and rope. While such activities can result in team members having more positive attitudes toward one another, there may be little impact upon how effectively the team actually works together. Improvements in cohesiveness do not always lead to improvements in team task performance. Research suggests that it is continual interaction and effort by all team members that leads to improvements in team functioning, rather than "quick fix" bonding sessions.

More effective team building processes involve taking days out of the team's regular work specifically to focus on task performance. Suitable topics for discussion would include:

- *Recent team successes and difficulties*
- *Team objectives and their appropriateness*
- *The roles of team members*
- *Quality of team communication*
- *Team meetings (frequency, content and value)*
- *Team decision-making*
- *Organizational support for innovation*
- *Conflict resolution in the team*
- *Organizational support for skill development*

INTERVIEWING AND RECRUITING

People are by far the most valuable asset of any team-based organization, so the process of interviewing and recruiting new team members is a crucially important one. If you are setting up a new team, you might consider asking someone from your organization's human resources department, if it has one, to help you draw up a list of criteria and sit in on the interviews. If you are recruiting candidates to join an established team, take some time with existing team members to list the criteria for selecting the new recruit. The people already in your team are ideally placed to know what skills and experience are required; by including them in this process you will demonstrate that you value their opinion and increase the chances of the new member being integrated into the group quickly and smoothly. With your team, list the technical skills the new person will need to play a full role, followed by the type of work experience that would be most relevant to the team's task. You should also consider what kind of person will offer a good fit or bring a fresh perspective, making the group more balanced (see pp.66–9).

Devise an advertisement that gives clear information about the job content and requirements, in order to only attract people with the skills you need. Then, together with your team if possible, select for interview those candidates that seem a good fit in terms of skills, and whose applications are carefully drafted. Set up the interview well in advance so that the candidate can prepare and make travel arrangements.

Ideally, you and two or three other team members should interview the candidates and then independently rate each

person against the criteria you started out with. You and your colleagues need to meet before the interview to decide which questions to ask the candidate and agree who will ask them (see box, below). Interviewees are more creative and responsive if you put them at ease by greeting each person warmly, holding the interview in a pleasant environment and starting and finishing on time. Always conclude by giving the candidate an opportunity to ask his or her own questions.

The main aim of the interview process is to select the candidate who will best enable the team to do its work successfully. Therefore, once the interviews are complete your interviewing team should discuss the pros and cons of each interviewee, weighing everything against the most important criteria and trying to arrive at a consensus. Offer your views last to avoid influencing the process too much.

KEY QUESTIONS

As most interviews are conducted within predetermined time limits, it is vital to ask the right questions. These lines of inquiry are most fruitful:

- **Why do you want to work in this team?**
  Is it for people reasons or task reasons? What other options were available to the candidate?
- **What experience do you have that is relevant to this team's work?**
  Look for similarities that might be disguised by, for example, the different nature of goals, or by different types of product.
- **What are the most important things that good teamworkers do?**
  Is their focus on reaching agreement, cooperating, getting the job done or communicating well? Explore the last three.
- **In the past, when you have disagreed with a team member, how have you dealt with this?**
  Answers will reveal their approach to diversity, and whether they can resolve and learn from differences of perspective.

PERSONALITY AND TEAMWORK

Effective team performance can be influenced by the mix of personalities in the team. As manager, it is your job to achieve the right balance of personalities so the team performs its job well.

Analysis of personalities can be done through personality models administered via questionnaires or psychometric tests. These should be carried out in collaboration with a trained professional who can advise you. Although people taking such tests tend to display a combination of personality dimensions, the results do highlight each individual's relative strengths.

The Myers Briggs Type Indicator is a personality measure that is used to achieve team compatibility by analyzing the cognitive styles of members. It describes the following scales: Extraversion–Introversion; Sensing–Intuition; Thinking–Feeling; and Judging–Perceiving. An alternative measure, the "Big Five" model, describes five personality dimensions: Openness to experience (such as a capacity for fantasy, actions and ideas); Conscientiousness (competence, order and self-discipline); Extraversion (positive emotions, gregariousness and warmth); Agreeableness (trust, straightforwardness and tender-mindedness); and Neuroticism (anxiety, self-consciousness and vulnerability). The particular dimensions that are most important in members of a team essentially depend on the type of task the team performs. If your team is primarily a decision-making body then people with high levels of extraversion are best because their warmth and optimism helps them to persuade others to accept their decisions. People tending towards neuroticism – who are good at judging risk – would be the most appropriate choice for a team that functions in a high-risk environment, such as a nuclear power station, or an action crew, such as a fire-fighting unit.

Some team managers try to build a balance of personality characteristics into their teams in order to ensure that each orientation is represented. Although, as a rule, personality traits should match the requirements of the task, a mix of personalities is also important. If your team is made up of strong, dominant people, you will probably have to manage a good deal of hostility, as several similar personalities will be in direct competition. Likewise, if you have a team of talented, creative, temperamental individualists, they will probably be good at coming up with innovative ideas, but not very effective at implementing them.

You cannot construct the ideal team of personalities. What is important is that you manage the team in a way that ensures that the personality mix is a source of creativity and energy, rather than hostility and conflict. If your team performs well and is effective, its members will like each other and be highly loyal; personality differences will not be a significant concern. Much of the advice given in this book focuses on how you can encourage your team to perform effectively – good interpersonal relationships will follow.

FOCUS AND VALUES:
CREATING A TEAM IDENTITY

You and your team members will work most effectively together if you share a positive sense of team identity. We all find meaning in our lives from the groups to which we belong – our family, our social networks, our workmates. In a work team, as in any other group activity, a shared sense of identity helps to create cohesion and direction. To foster such an identity is a key task for you as team manager. And one way to perform this task is to discover and foster the key *values* of the team. Values give meaning and focus to team activities, and shape the team's identity. And the values your team members bring to their work will influence the effort they put into it – which is why it is crucial for you as team manager to understand and support those values.

One way to gain this understanding is to ask individuals within the team what really matters to them at work. Do this regularly as the team evolves with the arrival of new members. After hearing the initial responses, try to probe more deeply by asking people the following specific questions:

"What are the times in your work life when you have felt fulfilled, in tune, in flow, and fully committed? What were you doing? What made that so special? What did it give you a chance to be, feel, become?"

Consider the themes that emerge from these individual conversations. Try to extract the common values that team members have expressed, and to summarize the results. Once you have succeeded in getting people to be honest about their needs, values and what they want from the team, you

can work with everyone, if necessary, toward reconciling the outlook of the team with that of strong-minded individuals. A team might value not only what it does (its contribution to the organization, or perhaps to society), but also the *way* in which it operates, or the challenges it faces. The experience of working together toward a mutual goal might, for some team members, be paramount.

Certain values can be expressed within almost any context – excellence in the work, respect for the people involved, the personal development and well-being of team members, and so on. For example, a team engaged in debt-collecting may value treating all the individual debtors with respect and consideration.

After taking your soundings among team members, share the key values that you discerned with the team. Then, work with the team to establish a set of norms or groundrules (see Work Solution 9, opposite). Encourage members to use these points as a touchstone – to review, as work progressses, whether the team continues to uphold its values.

You can also help to build team identity in less explicit ways. These might include participating in long-standing jokes, storytelling and jargon, as well as rituals, such as celebrating team members' birthdays. Another positive element in the social climate of a team is non-aggressive humour – a form of creative play, which can help to foster an ethos of innovation. All these aspects of the team's identity will create a positive atmosphere and encourage members to be committed to each other.

Other approaches to creating a strong group identity include parties, lunches, shared activities such as fitness routines, group jogging, and mixed football games. Encourage your team to get together from time to time at social functions, to enjoy a theatrical or musical evening, or an occasional day at the races. Such non-work activities promote a sense of identity and camaraderie.

When combined with success at work – the best way to cement team identity – all these cohesive factors will operate together to make the team an effective community.

WORK SOLUTION 9

Laying down the groundrules

You can greatly reinforce a team's sense of identity and shared values by establishing clear groundrules (explicit norms of conduct), which everyone is asked to agree and adhere to. Hold a team meeting in which to draw up these groundrules. As manager your job is to facilitate the process, encouraging members to focus on the essentials and draft a mutually agreed document.

1. Ask each individual team member to write up to four key norms in answer to the questions "What must we do?" and "What must we not do?", based on the team's shared values. Examples might be: "We will always work to the highest standards to meet our clients' needs"; "We will never keep customers waiting more than 24 hours for an answer to their queries"; or "We will always support each other's need to work flexible hours."

2. Collect all the statements and call a special meeting to discuss them one by one. Ask people to vote for the five statements they most agree with and also to vote on the order of their importance. If it seems appropriate, feel free to accept fewer or more statements, but do not exceed seven.

3. In the same meeting, write each agreed statement on a flipchart, in the order determined by the team. Go through the set of statements one by one and work together on refining them, or altering the order, where necessary.

4. After the meeting, present the finalized set of statements in a series of succinct bullet points, and issue them as the team's groundrules. These are the beacons to guide the team's activities and to set the tone for the work ahead. Display the groundrules in a communal area and give each team member a copy.

ESTABLISHING TEAM ROLES

To get the job done, team members need to understand the role that each person has within the team, and the tasks he or she is responsible for. To take just one obvious example, if there is confusion about who deals with customer complaints, there is a risk that they will never get answered.

Initially, roles will need to be defined by appropriately matching individual skills with the tasks to be done, as described in the work solution opposite. Breaking the tasks down into sub-tasks makes this easier. As team manager it is your job to ensure that everyone clearly understands how their individual objectives relate to overall team objectives, and also (this is subtly different) how their performance relates to overall team performance over time.

As the team's function develops, it will be helpful to have a team review meeting (say, six-monthly) to check that members' skills are being effectively deployed and that responsibilities are fairly and equally distributed. This meeting should be an open discussion of roles, responsibilities, objectives and workload distribution, looking into the future to see where overload is likely to occur and then making any necessary adjustments to ensure that no individual is overburdened. Encourage people to offer their help at such meetings: volunteers tend to work more conscientiously and contentedly than conscripts. Be sure that all such offers of good "citizenship" receive appropriate thanks.

WORK SOLUTION 10

Role clarification

If the team is to function effectively, the team manager must get individual members to participate constructively and cooperatively in the allocation of responsibilities. Perform this exercise in a team meeting at the start of the team's life, and again at six-monthly intervals as part of the role review process.

1. Begin by defining the team task and writing it as a single short statement on a flip-chart for team members to see. Ask team members to suggest the sub-tasks of the main task. Working together, refine these suggestions to create a clearly defined set of sub-tasks with which all members agree. Write these sub-tasks beneath the main team task. If the task is particularly complex, you may need to sub-divide the sub-tasks.

2. Ask each team member in turn to come forward and draw circles around the sub-tasks they believe that they are responsible for – either as a natural function of their roles or by previous agreement. Each team member should use a different shade of felt-tip pen to make the annotation clearer.

3. Discuss and debate any issues arising with everyone concerned – for example, roles unaccounted for, or overlap (where more than one team member has claimed a sub-task). Aim to clarify any confusion and to make precise demarcations between roles.

4. Once you have clarified all the roles to everyone's satisfaction, summarize the collective decisions that you have made. After the meeting, devise and circulate a graphic summary of who is responsible for each sub-task.

IMPROVING COMMUNICATION
WITHIN THE TEAM

Effective communication within the team is vital for successful team functioning, ensuring that everybody has the information they need to perform their roles and coordinate their activities with others. In the modern working world, we tend to be deluged with information – much of it inappropriate to our needs. So the main challenge of communicating within the team consists of assessing who needs what information, when, and in what form.

Information is valuable only when it confirms or alters the understanding of the team as a whole or of individual members – and the more it alters understanding, the richer it is. Empty information is not only irrelevant, it is a positive hindrance and potentially a great time-waster. The most effective teams will pass useful information to each other at appropriate times – sometimes concise, sometimes full of detail, according to need.

To answer the first parts of the above-mentioned question – who and what? – you and your team must understand the information needs of each member individually. Your role clarification meeting (see Work Solution 10, p.79) will have given members a clear view of their responsibilities, and from here it is a logical progression to ask members to be specific about what information they need and when they need it in order to perform their role.

To support this, encourage team members to give each other regular feedback (see box, below) on whether they are getting enough of the right information at the right time – or too much of the wrong information, or the right information too late. Consider setting aside specific times for members to do this – perhaps once a month at the start of team meetings. The same session should also cover the *form* in which people would like their information – whether in writing (via email or on paper) or orally (by phone, video-conferencing or in person).

Email is often used as a back-up or reminder, or as a system of minuting – which is fine, so long as the reminder doesn't disappear from sight, and so long as the minute gets filed as a printout. Email is usually the perfect medium for

FEEDBACK

Feedback consists of clear information about the consequences (whether positive or negative) of our actions or attitudes, which enables us to monitor our effect on others. Within teams, feedback is a vital form of communication that enables members to improve their own performance – and therefore the success of the team as a whole. By constantly delivering feedback yourself, and exhorting everyone else to do the same, you can create a climate in which feedback is regularly exchanged within the team. As we all learn faster and more lastingly from positive messages, encourage team members to focus primarily on giving positive rather than negative feedback: a ratio of something like 9:1 will usually be productive. Where negative feedback is appropriate, comments need to be constructive and sensitively expressed to preserve good working relationships. This means dispassionately describing actions and their consequences – what works, what doesn't work – rather than making sweeping personal judgments or flying off the handle.

communicating small amounts of information; while large amounts of factual information are better sent as email attachments that can be printed out by the recipient for perusal at their leisure. However, email is disastrous for managing conflicts, and weak as a way of sorting out complex problems or decision-making. Discourage your team from *ever* sending angry emails to each other.

As the richness of information depends on the extent to which it alters understanding, paper and email offer the least rich medium for transferring information because they are one-dimensional. Slightly richer are telephone conversations and video-conferencing. Richest of all is face-to-face communication, where vocal inflexion, facial expression and body language provide multiple channels of communication. Direct conversation offers the best forum for asking questions, exploring issues in depth, and sorting out disagreements, so teams should meet no less than once a month.

An *open flow* of communication is desirable, and this is part of the value of team meetings. Otherwise there is a risk that too much communication will go through you (causing a bottleneck), or that team members will talk primarily with the colleagues they get along with best. Regular social events help to open out social connections within a team, as well as offering a vehicle for useful communication and the building of trust and cohesion. Encourage team members to develop the core communication skills described on pp.52–7. To do this, model these skills yourself and persuade the team to set explicit norms of open and supportive communication.

WORK SOLUTION 11

Processing information usefully

Raw information often needs to be filtered, summarized or interpreted before it becomes useful to another team member or to the team as a whole. Or it may not be intelligible at all without supplementary information to make sense of it. Below are some questions to consider before passing on written or electronic information to others. Encourage your team to take these issues into account in their regular communications with you and with each other.

1. In what forum will the information be assessed? By an individual team member with time to study it in detail? Or by people in a meeting? In a meeting, people might find it more valuable to have a summary of the main points than the whole document. If so, consider who would be able to draw out the most significant points in a summary: knowing what to extract from the document might require a certain amount of specialist knowledge.

2. Will people understand the significance of the document or will this need to be pointed out to them – perhaps in a separate note?

3. Will people need a generous amount of time to study the information before it is discussed in a meeting? Ensure that no one is given too little time for the assessment required of them.

4. Will people know what level of response they need to give – first impressions or a more substantial analysis? Make sure that everyone knows what you expect.

5. If a failure to comment on the document means that it will be acted upon automatically, does everyone know this? Make sure that everyone understands the consequences of saying nothing.

CREATING AN ATMOSPHERE OF WARMTH AND SUPPORT

Psychological research has revealed repeatedly that when people are placed in a positive environment of interpersonal warmth and support, they behave cooperatively and altruistically, and think more creatively. Conversely, if people feel threatened, they adopt an attitude of aggression or defensiveness. As cooperation between members is crucial to effective team functioning, it makes sense to promote warmth and support within your team.

Support is the help that we offer to others and is therefore integral to the spirit of cooperation. There are four different types of support: emotional, instrumental, informational and appraisal. Emotional support involves listening to someone's troubles and offering empathy and understanding. Instrumental support consists of doing something practical for someone, such as taking on one of their assignments

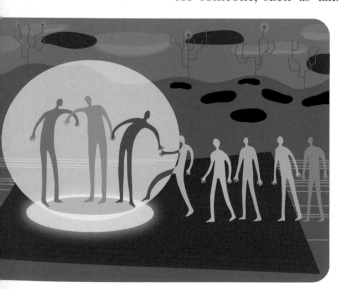

when they are overloaded. Informational support involves finding out information that will help someone do their work. Appraisal support provides feedback or advice that helps to make sense of someone's problems.

As part of your coaching role, make an effort to take time to speak regularly to all members on a one-to-one basis so that you keep in touch with their needs

WORK SOLUTION 12

Building two-way relationships

As team manager you need to encourage two-way rather than one-way relationships. When a relationship is one-way, the recipient often feels uncomfortable. It helps if individuals are made aware of the particular strengths that they are perceived as having. Knowing that their strengths may be called upon by other team members at any time, individuals are less likely to feel awkward when asking for help.

1. Work together as a team to identify each individual's strengths by applying the classification of team members devised by Dr R. Meredith Belbin, summarized below.

2. Make sure that everyone knows which slot they are perceived as filling. (Of course, this classification can also be helpful in the selection process.)

Plant – the ideas person, valued for their creativity.

Resource Investigator – the extrovert, valued for their contacts as well as their ability to develop ideas.

Monitor Evaluator – the analyst, valued for their shrewdness and prudence.

Shaper – the catalyst, valued for their dynamism and their challenging ideas.

Coordinator – the enabler, valued for their ability to ensure that others' talents are used most effectively.

Implementer – the focuser, valued for their practicality and their ability to focus on a task.

Completer Finisher – the perfectionist, valued for attention to detail as well as nervous energy.

Teamworker – the spearhead, valued for their hard work and people skills.

Specialist – the technician, valued for their knowledge and experience.

and offer support when appropriate. As well as informal chats around the office, set aside time specifically to check on the well-being of each individual. Ask them how they are getting on with their work and whether there are any problems that they would like to discuss. Encourage them to ask you for a specific form of help if they need it, reassuring them that you perceive such requests as practical and constructive rather than a sign of weakness. Where possible, establish an open-door policy so that members can come and speak to you whenever they need to.

By supporting team members yourself, you will help to establish a norm of supportive behaviour within the team. You can bring this norm into team consciousness by creating opportunities for the regular exchange of support within the team: create a formal slot during meetings in which all team members, including you, can take it in turns to request practical, informational or appraisal support from other team members; arrange regular social gatherings in which members can offer each other emotional support.

Demonstrations of warmth and caring toward the team from you and the wider organization can also do much to promote a positive and therefore productive working atmosphere. As manager you will probably be in a good position to put pressure on the organization to provide small perks, such as free supplies of tea, coffee and filtered water, and even larger benefits, such as gym membership, private health-care or counselling services. Within the context of your team, you can promote goodwill with gestures as simple as celebrating birthdays with cards and cake, providing new recruits with personalized mugs and bringing treats back from trips, as well as with more extravagant gestures, such as occasional free massages, yoga classes and other holistic treatments.

Certain factors, such as frequent member changes, can destabilize the team's emotional climate and provoke anxiety and unrest. To prevent these emotions from sabotaging the team climate, allow them to be acknowledged and expressed through appropriate rituals, such as leaving parties, welcome lunches and celebrations of team success at the end of a project. During projects, seek to stabilize team membership as much as possible. Where team members work in multiple teams or on short-lived project teams, set up a "home team" where they can touch base, get the social support that they need and discuss their learning requirements.

AVOIDING FAVOURITISM

Jealousy and rivalries between team members can powerfully disrupt a team's emotional climate, creating splits that hinder cooperation and team effectiveness. A common cause of jealousy within the team is preference shown toward certain team members by the manager. This behaviour creates an in-group and an out-group. In-group members are those you perceive to be more competent and likable; out-group members are those you think are less competent and more difficult to get on with. Team managers tend to attribute the successes of in-group members to their abilities and their failures to circumstances beyond their control; with out-group members they are likely to take the converse approach. Consider your relationship with your team members. Are there certain people that you spend more time with? If so, this may be creating resentment and jealousy in other members, who feel excluded. With this in mind, try to give equal attention and support to all. Coach those whose competence you feel less confident about. Develop your relationship with those who seem less agreeable.

chapter 4

TEAM PROCESSES

Once your team is up and running, your main role
as team manager is to ensure that team members
continue to operate together at maximum
effectiveness. This involves asking your team to
engage in a continual process of self-reflection in the
search for new and improved ways of doing things.

In this chapter we address the context and nature
of the main processes that take place within the team.
We begin by learning how to orient the team toward
an inspiring team vision with concrete objectives, to
give them clear direction for their activities. Then we
discover how to organize effective team meetings –
the forum in which many team processes take place.
To help run team meetings productively, we learn
strategies for encouraging full participation from all
members. We also discover how to improve ongoing
team processes, such as information sharing, progress
reporting and the coordination of activities, as well as
innovative techniques for solving problems, making
decisions and planning. In addition, we explore team-
based appraisal and reward systems, which promote
learning and development within the team.

SHAPING VISION AND OBJECTIVES

A compelling vision and concrete, achievable objectives that are in tune with the overriding goals of the organization are crucial to team success. Without them teams flounder, uncertain of their direction and lacking in motivation and a sense of purpose in their activities.

The task of shaping a vision lies primarily with the manager – it cannot be wholly democratic. However, managers can invite input from the team, and in any case they must obtain the support of all team members for the vision if it is to be effective. The first step is to identify precisely what the team is trying to achieve. To do this you must first consider a number of factors: the role of the team within the organization; the expectations of sponsors (who created the team) and stakeholders (those affected by the team's activities); the needs of customers or clients; and the performance of competitors. Your purpose is to respond to such external pressures effectively. Therefore, your vision must accommodate these demands while offering motivating challenges to the team.

Once you have devised a vision, the next step is to translate this into a clear, concise statement. To engage your team, the statement must be concrete, inspiring and consequential – qualities demonstrated in this statement by the manager of a pensions advisory team: *"It is our intention to provide a service that pleasantly surprises clients who come to get advice on their pensions. We will achieve this by focusing on their future needs and offering a variety of attractive options in ways that make sense to them."* This statement describes in concrete terms the desired outcome and how the team will achieve it. Rather than using uninspiring numerical targets, the outcome is expressed qualitatively by describing how the result feels (in this case to the customer). And because the values team members bring to their work influence the effort they put into it, the vision statement incorporates a shared sense of values — helping others, providing excellent service, being easily understood.

Once you have formulated a vision statement, ask the team for their opinions. If there is a general feeling that the wording should be altered, and this seems appropriate, modify it accordingly. As your team and its environment evolve during the team's lifespan, review the team vision statement on a regular basis to ensure that it continues to represent the purpose and values of the team. Otherwise, your vision may become a straitjacket that prevents the team from developing in new directions.

Team objectives specify how the vision will be put into practice and provide tangible goals for members to aim for and chart their progress by. Limit the team to four or five objectives at a time, or members may become confused and unfocused in their efforts.

To be effective, objectives should be specific, measurable, challenging and scheduled. This means stating them clearly, in numerical form (where possible), within a specified time-frame. For example, the objective for a telesales team might be to *"Boost monthly sales figures from cold-calling by 20 per cent by the end of the year"*. This statement clarifies what the team needs to achieve by a certain deadline, enabling them to see if and when they have failed, or are likely to fail, so that steps can be taken to remedy the situation. The focus of the objective in this example is an increase in productivity. Alternative markers of team success might include improvements in customer ratings, the gathering of information, or the development of skills or a product. There might also be subsidiary objectives that further the main objective – such as improvements in inter-team communication. Whatever the focus of your team's objectives, it is vital that they are realistic. Otherwise, team members will struggle to achieve them and lose confidence in their abilities.

Objectives should be set when your team first forms, or begins a new phase or project, and if necessary redefined at team appraisal meetings (see pp.112–14). Formulate objectives together with your team (see Work Solution 13, opposite) – it is the team who will be carrying out the work necesssary for achieving the objectives, so it is important that they have a say in what they are.

WORK SOLUTION 13

Setting objectives

Vision can be seen (and even represented graphically) as the trunk of a tree growing from its roots in the values, skills, beliefs and understanding of the team members. The team objectives are then the main branches of the tree, which produce the action plans (the twigs). You and your team can work out your objectives directly from the team vision or mission statement.

1. Once the vision statement has been agreed with the team, break it down with them into its key elements and, to begin with, try to ascribe one or two objectives to each element. Debate these objectives with the team and make any necessary adjustments. The aim should be to arrive at four or five outline objectives.

2. Discuss and debate ways to make the objectives measurable. For example, if you are aiming to increase customer service, you might choose to rate customer satisfaction on a scale of 1 (very dissatisfied) to 5 (very satisfied) and aim to raise average ratings from, say, 3 (neither satisfied nor dissatisfied) to 5.

3. Your objectives will mostly include a schedule and budget requirement. As well as setting acceptable targets for each, set optimum targets that present the team with a motivating challenge.

4. Consider with your team whether to set team functioning objectives – for example, a big increase in cooperation with other teams or with specific departments, especially those with which your team often finds itself in conflict. These objectives also may benefit from being quantified: again, use a numerical scale to grade subjective judgments.

MANAGING MEETINGS

Meetings provide the forum for most team processes, so it is vital that they take place regularly (at least once a month). To be effective, they must have a clear purpose: ask yourself what you are trying to accomplish. If the sole purpose is to share information, you may in theory be able to replace the meeting with an email exchange, but bear in mind the advantages of personal contact, debate, shared reflection and instant feedback. Consider who should attend: the scope of meetings is very much determined by their composition. Prepare and distribute a written agenda (see Work Solution 14, opposite). Ensure that the venue is provided with all the relevant equipment and refreshments.

As manager you will normally facilitate or chair meetings, although you can delegate this role to others on occasion. Ensure that the meeting begins on time, and stick to the agenda as closely as possible. This will prevent unnecessary tangents, ensuring that the meeting fulfills its purpose and ends on time. Conclude with a summary of what has been agreed, making sure that everybody is clear about the tasks that they need to do before the next meeting.

It's important to be clear beforehand who will take minutes for the meeting. These should follow the agenda and detail, item by item, the decisions made and tasks allotted (with initials to indicate who will do them), with deadlines noted. There should always be a note on who was present – as a reminder that absentees will not have the complete picture. The minutes may also note issues to be covered in the next meeting, and give a provisional date for that meeting.

WORK SOLUTION 14

Setting an agenda

Setting a clear agenda is vital if your meetings are to be productive. Ask team members to submit to you any topics that they would like to see covered at the meeting a couple of days beforehand. Once you have collated this information, plan your agenda following the steps in this exercise.

1. At the top of the agenda, write the name of the team that will be meeting and the type of meeting if applicable. Then state the date and location, the start and finish times, and the name of the person who will be facilitating.

2. Summarize the main objectives of the meeting in one or two sentences, and list the desired outcomes for the meeting.

3. List the topics that need to be addressed during the meeting in a logical order. For each topic state the processes for working through it and who will be participating in those processes. For example, if a topic was "Select a company logo", the processes and participants might be: Present the prototypes – PR and Marketing director; Discuss and evaluate options – all team members; Reach agreement – all team members.

4. For each topic state approximate start and finish times. Although these should be flexible, they will help to keep the team focused on the task in hand and prevent you from including too many impromptu items. Also allow time for an introductory overview and a closing summary to be presented by the facilitator.

5. Present the agenda in a clear, readable format and distribute it to the team, preferably at least one day before the meeting.

ENCOURAGING PARTICIPATION

Central to the effective management of meetings, and indeed of teams in general, is the challenge of finding ways to maximize the participation of all involved. After all, one of the main reasons for teamworking is to benefit from the shared wisdom, knowledge and experience of everybody on the team. Not only this, but full participation from team members gives them a stake in the outcome of the team's work, boosting their commitment and motivation.

Full team participation is not simply a matter of consulting members and then making the decisions based on your own judgment. Nor does it involve total democracy whereby every decision is taken by a team vote, as this leads to decision-making paralysis rather than team effectiveness. In fact, the ideal is a mixture of approaches

Routine decisions will be taken by individuals according to a predetermined plan. When allocating roles and responsibilities (see pp.78–9), specify the brief for each team member, so that they are clear about the decisions they can take. At team meetings and reviews, give members the opportunity to report back on any important decisions they have taken, to keep everyone informed about what is happening within the team and offer an opportunity to iron out any problems.

Strategic or complex issues should be decided with the involvement of the whole team. As manager, you may be the main barrier to full team participation. You may dominate without even being aware of it, simply by virtue of your position. This is because people tend to take their cues from the top. Studies of team meetings have shown that managers typically speak more than anyone else, and what they say is listened to more carefully. Think back over the last time your team debated a complex issue. You may remember that you, as team manager, spoke first, and that when other team members voiced opinions it was in response to your comments more often than to anyone else's. You need to be aware of this effect and take steps to prevent it from inhibiting potentially useful contributions – for example, you might decide to ask team members to express their opinions before offering your own.

As well as the manager, overly confident or vociferous team members can dominate meetings by taking up disproportionate "airtime" or arguing so vigorously with the opinions of others that their own views prevail, regardless of their actual value. The best way to handle such individuals is to coach them privately during individual feedback sessions (see p.115) on the need to listen more. During meetings, you can interrupt talkative team members by summarizing what they have said so far and then inviting other team members to contribute. If the problem of dominance is really troublesome, you could open up a discussion about it in one of the team's regular review meetings.

The flip-side of this problem is the tendency for shy team members to hold back from expressing their opinions. To overcome this obstacle, try structuring the debate by requesting

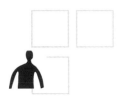

the opinion of each team member in turn: contrary to expectation, I have found that this often speeds up the decision-making process. Otherwise, what can happen is that resistance from quieter members is only revealed at the end of the discussion when the vote is taken. When this occurs you have to reopen the debate, or risk bad feeling and lack of commitment to the final decision if the dissent is ignored.

Another problem occurs when team members who lack communication skills are unable to present their views and knowledge successfully. In such cases it is your job to clarify an individual's opinion by first questioning them and then checking your understanding of their responses by reflecting back what you have heard (see pp.52–4). This approach ensures that each member's ideas are attended to by the team.

Conversely, someone skilled at "impression management", who can speak persuasively even though they may lack knowledge or expertise, can exert a disproportionate influence. In such situations try to ensure that other, more informed views, as well as all the necessary facts, are brought to the attention of the meeting.

Team members' participation should be real, not nominal. If you consult but never actually take account of others' views, they will stop participating. If they see that you value their contributions and implement their ideas (especially the ones that persuaded you from the course you originally advocated), they will feel highly motivated to contribute, as they will feel a sense of empowerment.

WORK SOLUTION 15

Step-ladder debating

Step-ladder debating encourages active participation by giving all team members the opportunity to offer solutions to a problem without placing them under pressure to conform. This approach maximizes the number of creative solutions that are presented to the team and leads to greater questioning of ideas, thereby improving the quality of decision-making and boosting commitment to the final decision. Use this technique for problems you think can be more easily solved by collective brainstorming.

1. First, give everybody within the team ten minutes to analyze the problem and come up with a list of two or more potential solutions on their own.

2. Then ask each team member to pair up with a partner. Request each pair to nominate a partner A and a partner B. Give partner A three minutes to present their solutions to partner B. During this time partner B may ask questions to clarify the information but not offer an opinion. Then give partner B three minutes to do the same with partner A. Next, give all the pairs five minutes to discuss their solutions with each other, together drawing up lists of the pros and cons of their respective solutions.

3. Allowing ten minutes, ask each pair to team up with another pair to present their solutions and discuss them with each other. When the time is up, ask each group to choose two of the best solutions raised within the group and present them to the rest of the team.

4. Ask each individual to select what they think is the best solution they have heard and explain why. Allow between 40 and 60 minutes to discuss the proposed solutions as a team before deciding which solution to implement.

CREATIVE PROBLEM-SOLVING

There are two important preliminary stages to problem-solving: the exploration of the problem and the generation of constructive ideas for solving the problem. These come before the stages of *selecting* the solution (which is covered on pp.104–107, under the heading of "Making decisions") and then *implementing* that solution.

Problem exploration involves establishing all the relevant facts, then trying out different ways of understanding the problem. Idea generation consists of pooling the ideas of team members to arrive at a repertoire of possible solutions. Teams need to engage thoroughly with both of the key preliminary stages to generate the maximum number of possible ways to tackle the problem, before going on to choose between them on the basis of pros and cons.

Often, when teams fail to find creative solutions to problems, it is because they have overlooked or underplayed the initial exploration stage, concentrating their efforts instead on

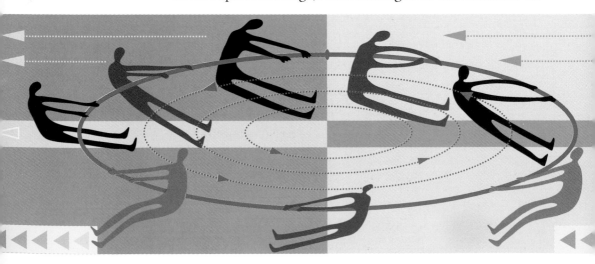

the search for solutions. Central to problem exploration is the process of uncovering all the relevant facts and bringing them to the attention of the whole team. This can be more difficult than you might expect: there is a tendency for teams to focus their full attention only on information that is shared between everyone prior to the discussion, and to ignore new information that emerges during the course of the debate. This tendency manifests itself even in those who introduce the new material into the group. Psychologists call this the "hidden profile phenomenon".

As team manager you can counter this effect by alerting the team to information held by only one or two members. Repeating the information yourself can be enough to bring it more prominently to the attention of the team, especially if you set it in relation to information that is already shared and then elucidate any implications it might have for the problem under discussion.

As well as examining the facts, it is helpful to consider a problem from different perspectives. This leads to a clearer understanding of the problem, and often points to creative ways to proceed. One valuable approach is to encourage your team to restate problems as a series of "How to ... ?" questions. For example, the problem of a competitor outselling you on one of your key products – a low-cost washing machine – could be restated as: How to reduce production costs in order to further lower the price? How to increase the impact of advertising? How to find out if the competitor's machine has features that are more popular with customers?

For a given problem, make a list of "How to … ?" questions on a flip-chart. Go through the list together with your team members, highlighting the questions that look as if they might lead to the most promising solutions.

Once the team has set itself a list of questions, it is in a strong position to generate solutions based on the facts available. A good way to handle this process is the step-ladder debating technique set out in Work Solution 15, p.99. To maximize the creative potential of the ideas that emerge, it is essential for the team to be open-minded and exploratory in its discussions. Make sure that the team spends enough time clarifying the key components of each possible solution and assessing its merits. Ask questions such as "How will this idea benefit our clients?" or "How will this plan help us to achieve our objectives?" Focusing on outcomes in this way will encourage the team to judge ideas on the basis of quality rather than on factors such as the status of the proposer.

Call upon all team members to respond to each proposal in turn. Ensure that everyone tries to give equal consideration to the pros and cons of each, and try to flush out any bias or ulterior motives that might creep into these assessments.

This approach ensures that team members listen to each other carefully and respectfully, encouraging even the most unforthcoming to express themselves freely. At the end of the discussion, the result should be a number of well-developed solutions. Write these on a flip-chart for everyone to see, then proceed to decision-making to decide which solution to implement (see pp.104–107).

WORK SOLUTION 16

Stakeholder analysis

Stakeholder analysis is a method of testing and improving proposed solutions prior to implementation. Stakeholders are all those interested parties who are affected by what the team does. By assessing how stakeholders will be affected by a solution, the team can anticipate any problems and resistance that may arise, and then look for creative ways to pre-empt those difficulties. Stakeholders are less likely to resist changes if they feel that creative thought has been put into how those changes will affect them.

1. On a flip-chart, list all the solutions generated by the team. Looking at each solution in turn, work with the team to identify the main stakeholders – these could be individuals, teams, departments, clients or customers. It could be that all the solutions will affect the same stakeholders; or alternatively it could be that some solutions will affect only *some* of the stakeholders.

2. With the team go through the advantages and disadvantages of each solution in relation to the stakeholders concerned. Put yourselves in the stakeholders' shoes: this will require an effort of imagination, and an understanding of what the stakeholders' priorities will be. If a team member is especially well-placed to understand these priorities, ask for his or her input on the question.

3. Then go through the same process modifying each solution, if appropriate, to ensure that it is likely to be more acceptable to the stakeholders concerned. Are there any ways to cushion the impact or introduce compensatory factors?

4. Take note of any stakeholders who seem to be particularly disadvantaged by the most plausible solutions. Exploring the implications at this stage can be helpful in any future conflict with the stakeholders concerned.

Having generated a number of creative solutions to a problem, the next task is to choose which one to implement. The success of the solution will depend largely upon the commitment of those responsible for its implementation, and for this reason it is vital to reach a decision that all the team members support.

One way to bring about such a consensus is to reinforce the team's shared sense of purpose. To this end, when team members present the cases for particular solutions, request them to do so in relation to agreed goals and values by asking questions such as: "What goals would your choice of supplier help us to achieve?" or "We are committed to maintaining high levels of customer service – would your proposal enable us to do this?" Such questions draw the team into areas of common ground, directing their thoughts toward ways to achieve the best outcome for the team as a whole.

However, there is a pitfall in common ground, and that is "groupthink", a tendency for tightly-knit teams to make

mistakes in their decision-making because they are more concerned with reaching agreement than with the quality of the decisions made. This is particularly likely to occur where there is a strong leader and when debate is interpreted as personal criticism. (See pp.128–129 for advice on avoiding groupthink.) Another pitfall is "risky shift" – the tendency of teams to make more extreme decisions than individuals because no one person feels responsible for the decision. "Extreme" may mean more experimental or more conservative, depending on circumstances and the composition of the team. Managers should be aware of both pitfalls and take corrective measures when either of them begins to manifest itself.

An effective technique available to any team manager is the promotion of constructive controversy. In a climate of cooperation, respect and trust, where team members focus on achieving the best outcome for the team, critical review is seen as constructive rather than aggressive. This means that it can be routinely applied in a neutral and productive way to the opinions of all team members – a process that affirms rather than questions the competence of each individual (see Work Solution 17, p.107). Such constructive controversy leads to innovative decisions that are supported by the whole team.

Where there is an atmosphere of competition between members, teams find it very difficult to work together to find mutually acceptable solutions. This is because the competitive spirit places individual ambition before team objectives, to the extent that members will do almost anything to prove their arguments right. Taken to extremes, such conduct can lead team members to question the competence of their colleagues in order to assert the authority of their argument. At this point, constructive debate breaks down as disagreements become personal rather than professional. As team manager you must intervene to resolve such conflict before discussions get out of hand (see pp.126–7).

This type of conflict is based on a polarized win–lose mentality. Such logic argues that if you are right, I am automatically wrong, so to avoid feeling inferior I cannot allow you to be right. To counteract this type of thinking, you need to create a win-win culture within your team. In order to do this you must reward cooperative rather than competitive behaviour. You can do this quite simply by praising team members for their constructive contributions to the discussion – making it clear that those who are skilled in winning arguments are not going to win support through eloquence alone. Implementing some of the team-based reward systems described on pp.116–19 will further reinforce this message.

Having established the facts, you are in a position to explore the common ground shared by opposing viewpoints. Ask the team as a whole to identify the points that are agreed upon – these could be facts, priorities, or preferred courses of action. Building on this foundation, you and your team can then work to integrate the opposing positions to develop a single solution that everybody supports.

One way to do this is to ask each faction to suggest creative ways of developing their proposal in a way that would meet or exceed the underlying objectives of their opponents. This encourages the two sides to develop a convergent solution – a creative combination of ideas from both sides that wins consent. Once a solution has been decided upon, the team is ready to put in place a plan of implementation.

Two-stage brainstorming

Studies have shown that individuals separately initiating and then pooling ideas will often come up with thinking that is superior in quality and quantity to the collective ideas of the whole team working together. If we are in a group I can't think while you are telling me your ideas, and in my response I might well be influenced to choose a route not far removed from yours. The following brainstorming exercise combines the best of both worlds – highly individual (even wild) creativity combined with the testing and refining process that stems from well-directed teamwork. The group discussion piggybacks on individual creativity and generates a sense of fun.

1. Gather together the team and ask each individual to work alone for five minutes, on a sheet of paper writing down their ideas on the subject in question and dividing them into two categories: left-brain (logical) and right-brain (intuitive). Tell everyone to be as profuse as they can, and not to worry if some of their thoughts seem impracticable or over-ambitious.

2. After the 5 minutes are up, collect the sheets of paper, shuffle them and hand them out at random, one to each team member. Ask the team members in turn to read aloud the proposed ideas they have been given.

3. After all the ideas have been read out, debate them freely, looking at the pros and cons of each. It is expressly understood that no one will be blamed for any ideas that get rejected when the necessary decisions are finally made: all that matters is that everyone is allowed their say.

4. As team manager, summarize the general view reached after the debate, and state the decisions that have emerged. Take a vote if opinion is evenly divided.

PLANNING PROCESSES AND RISK MANAGEMENT

Planning takes place at all levels and stages of activity throughout the course of a team's life and is important as a way to make sure that the team achieves its goals – on schedule and (if applicable) on budget. The degree of detail in the planning is critical to success. Too little, and you are at the mercy of unforeseen complications. Anything could happen to throw your project off course – including insufficient resources, excessive demands placed on outside suppliers, key people required to do too much within the organization, or incompatibility of technology between different systems. Too much planning, on the other hand, and you run the risk of getting bogged down in unnecessary detail, without any corresponding gains. Excessive planning tends to create rigidity where there should be flexibility.

The most effective planners identify and schedule the steps to be taken to reach the goal, while allowing sufficient flexibility to work around the variables – whether in the organization itself or in the industry as a whole. If the timing of a particular phase of action is uncertain, then ideally the plan makes allowance for this. The final result of the planning process is a schedule, which is usually created and monitored within a computer spreadsheet. It is a good idea to display a printout of at least the outline schedule on the team noticeboard for all to see. Marking off the stages as they are achieved, on or off schedule, highlights the team's achievements or focuses everyone's mind on time pressures – depending on whether the project runs according to plan.

Many projects overrun on either schedule or budget, or both. Often, the two factors are related: either a delayed completion date results in extra costs, or else a cost shortfall takes time to resolve (for example, by raising more cash from investors), with consequent damage to the schedule. When a schedule extension breaks budget, often this is solely to do with the additional staff costs – "people over time". The number of months of overrun

multiplied by the monthly salary multiplied by the number of people in the team can amount to a formidable sum. This points to the vital need for all team managers with budgetary responsibilities to be acutely sensitive to the risks of falling behind schedule. A regular cost-monitoring operation should be established, and all team members should report on their progress and spending on a regular basis – as well as being aware of any permissable margin for error either in schedule performance or budget performance.

One of the team manager's responsibilities, not only at the planning stage but all the way through the team project, is to manage what is known as the "project triangle" – the interrelationship of time, cost and performance (where performance is a quality of service or the specifications for a product). These are often the three main factors that will be stated or implied in the team's vision statement, although the emphasis will vary according to the team's activities. Ensure as team manager that you understand how the three factors impact upon one another, and plan accordingly.

An important aspect of planning, and one that should also be subject to continual review, is risk management. Within the context of a team, this is a process that aims to make team members aware of what can go wrong and enable them to assess the impact of various possible scenarios and act accordingly. The appropriate action is either to avert the risk if this is deemed to be a realistic prospect or to make contingency plans if members feel that some of the risk is bound to materialize. Examples of possible outcomes that need to be considered in relation to a new team project might include: Does the project use new technologies that members have not used before? Are there untested safety implications in the construction of the project? In the event of failure or poor press coverage, would the activities of the wider organization be adversely affected? Sometimes risks will need to be weighed against each other, and many team managers find it helpful to devise a numerical scale for a comparative assessment of this kind. Bear in mind that some measure of risk is a necessary sign of positive enterprise. A risk-free environment, in the commercial world at least, is an impossibility.

WORK SOLUTION 18

Managing the risks

When managing a team you can be fairly sure that, at some point, something will happen that hampers progress. However, if you take time to consider the foreseeable risks at the planning stage, you will often be able to avert them or make contingency plans to handle them. This exercise takes you through the process of managing risks, which should be started at the planning stage.

1. First identify the risks that might adversely affect the team's work. To do this consider each of the following categories of problems: interpersonal (problems in relationships within the team or between team and organization); material (problems with the supply of resources that the team needs to function); operational (problems with the systems and processes of teamworking).

2. Quantify each risk. First consider the negative impact it would have on the project if it were to happen, classifying it as "high", "moderate" or "low". Then assess the probability that each will occur, classifying it as "high, "moderate" or "low".

3. Based on your quantification of each risk, decide which ones to manage.

4. For those risks that you decide to manage you have four options: transfer the risk by giving it to someone else (for example, by insuring it); avoid the risk by altering your plans to take an alternative course of action; reduce either the probability or the impact of the risk by taking appropriate measures; accept the risk and draw up contingency plans if possible.

5. When reviewing the progress of your plans, reassess your risk list in the light of changing circumstances and make any necessary changes to your plans.

CONDUCTING APPRAISALS

Appraisals are the primary tool for reviewing the performance of the team and resetting objectives. They provide the opportunity to look at and learn from failures and successes, and therefore play an important role in supporting the team's ongoing development. Essentially, there are two types of appraisal – team appraisal and individual appraisal. Both should take place regularly – at least once or twice a year, but more frequently if your team is relatively short-lived.

Team appraisals

It is the team manager's role to lead team appraisals and facilitate team members' contributions in an atmosphere of openness and mutual respect. Beforehand, ask everyone in the team to prepare for the appraisal by privately assessing the team's performance in the following areas: achievement of vision and objectives; team viability; team innovation; and inter-team relations.

As each of these areas require different forms of evaluation, you must first define the assessment criteria for each one so that all team members are working from a common perspective. The *team vision* is qualitative rather than quantitative, so bear in mind that assessments of how well the team has so far achieved its vision will be based on subjective feelings rather than concrete evidence. By contrast, *team objectives* are measured according to concrete criteria for success, which you and your team can evaluate more objectively.

Team viability depends on the quality and sustainability of team relationships. To assess this aspect of performance, the

team should reflect on the prevalence of supportive, cooperative attitudes (such as offers by people to assist each other), which suggest sustainable relationships; and criticism, intolerance and competition, which indicate poor relationships.

Innovation, or creativity, is an excellent barometer of team functioning. As this can be an elusive quality, it is best assessed in terms of results – ideally, new and improved ways of doing things. As a team consider the innovations introduced since the last appraisal, and how productive they have been.

The efforts of teams should be directed toward organizational goals, which means that *inter-team relations* are critical markers of success. To enable the team to evaluate such relations, request feedback from other managers, either formally with a questionnaire, or informally at interdepartmental meetings. Make this feedback available to team members.

At the start of team appraisals, ask each team member in turn to deliver their assessment of the team's performance in each of these key areas by giving comments as well as a specific grade or score relating to the predetermined criteria. Then deliver your own assessment. When you and your team have identified the team's successes and failures in each area, analyze the assumptions, actions and/or processes that led to them. This information will enable your team to evolve in the future by replicating what works and eradicating what doesn't. To reinforce such changes it may help to redefine the team objectives (see pp.92–3).

Individual appraisals

In most organizations, team managers have sole responsibility for giving appraisals to team members and helping them to set personal objectives for the coming year. However, in the intimacy of the team environment, individual appraisals are more effective when feedback comes from the entire team. Under this arrangement all team members are asked to review each person in terms of their contribution to the team by evaluating (with a grade and written comments) the following factors as objectively as they can: productivity, role performance, communication, participation in team processes, planning, conflict resolution, innovation, and supportiveness. Team members can then help each other to define their personal goals for the following year (see box, opposite).

In long-standing teams that have developed strong, supportive relationships between members, the best way to present members' views is in an open forum. However, where people feel uncomfortable being subjected to public scrutiny, opt initially for the less threatening option of asking people to supply a written review for each of the other team members, taking into account all the above areas. You can then collate the information before relaying it to individual team members on a one-to-one basis. This allows you to mediate the feedback, ensuring that it is constructive and supportive. In private you can discuss the feedback between you, decide what the team member can do to improve his or her performance and set goals for doing so.

Overall, the individual appraisal process should help members to clarify their objectives, ensure that they feel valued, respected and supported by the team, and help them to identify ways to achieve personal development.

SETTING PERSONAL GOALS

The setting of personal goals for each team member is an important part of the individual appraisal process. Goals should focus on the year ahead and possibly subsequent years. When setting personal goals, work through these steps with the team member concerned:

1. *Assess the needs of the "customer". This may be other team members, another team, the organization, or an external customer.*
2. *Describe the task of the individual team member.*
3. *Identify the individual stages or components of the task.*
4. *Bearing in mind any new findings from the individual appraisal, identify four or five personal goals for the year ahead.*
5. *Establish performance indicators (for example, customer satisfaction).*
6. *Establish measurement processes.*

Encourage team members to review their performance against these goals at regular intervals during the year and at individual appraisals.

REWARDS AND INCENTIVES

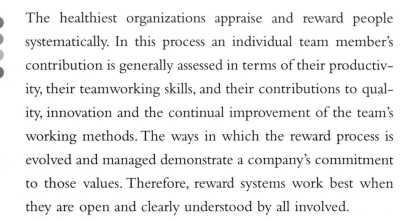

The healthiest organizations appraise and reward people systematically. In this process an individual team member's contribution is generally assessed in terms of their productivity, their teamworking skills, and their contributions to quality, innovation and the continual improvement of the team's working methods. The ways in which the reward process is evolved and managed demonstrate a company's commitment to those values. Therefore, reward systems work best when they are open and clearly understood by all involved.

The individual

Traditionally, appraisal processes concentrate on the individual rather than the team. However, in a team-based organization one way to assess an individual team member's performance is against a specific target in the context of the team's activities. It is not uncommon, as we have already seen (see p.114), for the team members themselves to be involved in carrying out this evaluation.

The team

Another approach entirely is the appraisal of collective effort in relation to team goals. In this case rewards may be distributed equally to each member of the team, or apportioned individually by senior management or the team manager; alternatively the distribution of rewards may be determined by the team itself.

It is important to note that where rewards are apportioned equally to team members by an external party, this can lead to considerable resentment. Those who do not pull their weight may well be regarded as benefitting unfairly from the compensatory efforts of their team-mates. And this may demotivate the people who are working the hardest. A process by which the team members themselves determine the distribution of team rewards available is more likely to be seen as a fair one.

The rewards allocated to individuals or teams will usually be a reflection to some extent of the performance of either the organization as a whole, or of a particular branch or division within it. A well-rounded reward system is one that incorporates all three of the elements referred to here – individual, team and organization. Where teamwork is an important ingredient of an organization's culture, it is desirable for its appraisal and reward system to place a strong emphasis on team perform-ance and, as much as possible, to delegate decisions about the distribution of rewards to the team members themselves.

Any successful reward system for a team-based enterprise will follow certain universal criteria:

• There should be clear, achievable but challenging targets, which all team members understand and, ideally, have a part in setting.

• There should be a clear and fair means of establishing the extent to which these targets have been met – that is, to measure success in relation to the team's goals.

• The system should recognize the extent to which the individuals within a team are dependent on each other – in other words, no one's contribution should be seen as exceptionally meritorious if in fact that contribution has been made possible only by the efforts of others.

• The team should be allowed a considerable degree of autonomy in the way in which it manages its work.

• The team should have access to the materials, skills and knowledge that it needs to achieve success.

• The reward should be commensurate with the scale of the team's achievement.

• The reward should be delivered soon after the appraisal has taken place.

The team and the individual

Any company with the task of designing a team-based reward system is entitled to ask, "How can we reward teams while still acknowledging the contribution made by individuals?" The answer will vary according to the company's level of commitment to the values of teamwork.

For example, one option might be to have two components within the package: an annual salary review related to inflation and organizational performance (but with no rewards for individual merit); and, added to that, a system whereby team members nominate each other to receive rewards for outstanding team performance. This second, team-related component need not be monetary: some organizations offer a variety of rewards from which employees can choose, such as travel passes, a case of wine, time off with pay, flexitime working, and so on.

Another possible formula, which might be appropriate in the world of retailing, would be for all salespeople whose teams had met their sales target for the year to receive a payrise equating to a fixed percentage of each individual's baseline pay; and, to supplement this, for the best-performing team to receive additional non-monetary rewards as well as a symbolic annual plaque.

HOW TO OPTIMIZE A REWARD SYSTEM

1. *Tailor rewards to the specific needs and values of your team rather than slavishly copying programs introduced elsewhere.*

2. *Create many winners and few losers by distributing rewards so that all or most team members are left feeling pleased, recognized and motivated. Any losers should be clear about why they have missed out.*

3. *Involve the team in the distribution of rewards by linking the reward system to a team-based appraisal system (see pp.112–15), which depends upon the input of all team members. Also, give members the opportunity to nominate teams and individuals for awards.*

4. *Combine financial incentives with non-monetary rewards ranging from the less expensive, such as words of appreciation, letters of congratulations, merchandise, gift vouchers and achievement certificates, to the more expensive, such as time off with pay, dinner for two, a company car, free travel, even a vacation.*

5. *Create flexibility by combining a few big awards offered on occasion with lots of small ones offered regularly. This gives scope for rewarding teams or individuals in accord with their achievements.*

6. *Communicate the structure and principles of the reward system to employees so that they understand it and feel motivated by it.*

chapter 5

TEAMS IN TROUBLE

While the benefits of teams are many and varied, it is important to realize that they carry a whole range of problems that are specific to teamworking. If you cannot resolve these problems, your team may not only fail to bring about the intended benefits but also prove destructive to members and the organization.

Teams comprise a group of people working together. Consequently, the problems from which they suffer are very human ones: people argue; members free-ride; teams opt for comfortable unity rather than risk the conflict of disagreement. In this chapter we begin by exploring the five main causes of failure in teams and how to avoid them. We go on to address the most common problems that arise within teams, learning how to identify them and what steps we can take to deal with them. These include "difficult people", who may be the symptom rather than the cause of the problem; interpersonal conflicts, which can destroy team relationships; the tendency for groupthink in tightly-knit teams; social loafing, when members don't pull their weight; and hidden defensive routines as a response to external threats.

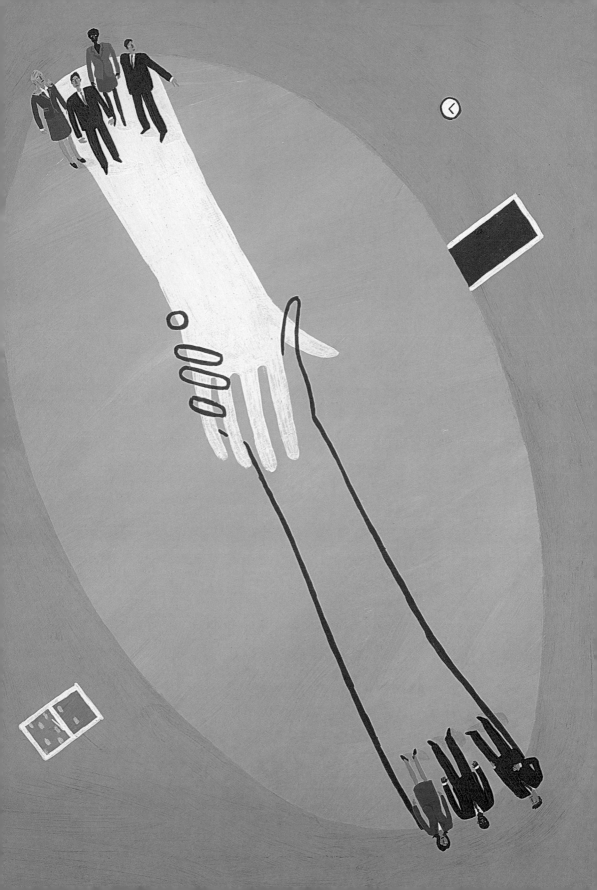

CAUSES OF FAILURE

Despite the many and varied benefits of teams, they also carry their fair share of problems, which, if left unresolved, can ultimately lead to team failure. However, most of these problems are caused by management mistakes and are therefore within your power to resolve.

Teams without tasks

The point of a team is to complete a task or meet a set of objectives. If you are keen to implement teams within your organization, you must first be sure that there is suitable work for the team to do. Forcing people into teams for the sake of it may actually do more harm than good, causing conflict, confusion and disruption within the organization.

Teams without freedom and responsibility

Creating teams and then failing to give them the freedom and authority to accomplish their tasks is akin to teaching your child to ride a bicycle, giving them a fancy racing bike and then telling them they can only ride it in their bedroom. For team members, the result will be frustration, disappointment and ultimately a loss of faith in the concept of teamwork. If you want your team to operate in an effective and creative way together, trust in their abilities and give them the authority and autonomy to do the job themselves.

Focusing on members, forgetting the team

If your management style tends to be oriented toward individuals rather than teams, you will encourage competitive, individualistic attitudes rather than cooperative team attitudes. For example, if you exclusively reward individual achievements rather than team effort, you are communicating the message that it is the individual, not the team, that is important. A radical reorientation of your approach toward team-based action will be needed if your team members are to subsume their individual identities within that of the team.

Team dictators, not managers

The strength of teams lies in the pooling of knowledge, skills and experience that they enable. If you apply a traditionally directive, even dictatorial, approach to your team, you will stifle its creativity. Instead, act as a facilitator for your team, supporting members in the early stages, coaching them to find the solutions for themselves and gradually slackening the controls as the team becomes more autonomous.

Strong teams in conflict

If you have developed an effective team, but it is unable to cooperate with other teams, it will still fail the organization. Working toward the success of the organization should be the overriding goal of both you and your team. Motivating your team by encouraging competition with other teams will cause it to develop into a rigidly insular group. Instead, promote team success as a step to organizational success. Encourage communication with other teams on a formal and informal basis and meet regularly with other team managers to find ways of improving the links between teams.

DIFFICULT PEOPLE

What do you do if there is a difficult member who seems to be disrupting the team's work? Before you act, think about *how* this person is difficult, and the reasons behind your perception. Could it be that the individual is in fact the victim of scapegoating? This is common when teams find themselves failing: instead of addressing the true cause, the team may unconsciously try to rid itself of problems by heaping blame onto one person and thus trying to drive him or her away.

Those who are in some way different from the rest of the team are often vulnerable to being labelled as difficult – the newcomer to a long-standing team, the lone woman in a team of men, the computer wizard in a team of techno-phobes. Yet the shift in perspective offered by these indiv-iduals can spark creativity, saving the team from its own homogeneity – but only if members value that difference. Likewise, those who disagree with the majority are often seen as being difficult. Yet teams that tolerate dissent are much more creative and innovative than those that do not. Con-

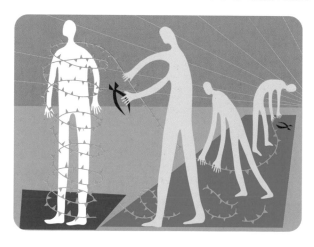

sider whether the so-called difficult individual is simply different or dissenting, and if so, encourage other team members to explore, value and be stimulated by their alterna-tive views (see p.102). The "difficult" person may turn out to be the most important member of the team.

Sometimes lack of understanding of an individual's role or contribution can cause other members to brand them as difficult. Clearly establishing the roles and responsibilities of each team member at the start of the team's life (see pp.78–9) will help to counter this effect. If a member's role changes at a later stage, it is vital to ensure that the rest of the team is aware of and understands the change.

Having considered these possibilities, you may conclude that the individual is genuinely difficult. He or she may be dominating, poor at communicating, aggressive, sarcastic or gruff. The way to deal with such personalities is to coach, rather than exclude. Spend time chatting with the person to see if you can locate the source of the problem. If they are poor communicators, coach them to improve their communication skills (see pp.80–83). Alternatively, they may feel alienated by the rest of the team. If so, take steps to integrate them by encouraging them to participate more in team activities – both at work and out of hours. Ask the rest of the team to support the individual's efforts by giving positive feedback in the form of appreciation and encouragement.

If all attempts to support someone in becoming more team-oriented fail, it may be that they do not share the team's values. If this is the case, their presence on the team will disrupt the team's work – a situation that should not be tolerated. In this event your only option may be to move them elsewhere in the organization or, if necessary, out of the company altogether. This is a radical situation: use it only when you have exhausted all possible alternatives.

INTERPERSONAL CONFLICT

Properly managed, conflict within a team can be a natural and healthy reflection of the diversity of its members, and a source of creativity and innovation in processes such as problem-solving and decision-making (see pp.100–107). However, when conflict becomes personal and members start attacking each other, it can destroy relationships and damage the effectiveness of the team.

When interpersonal conflicts arise, it is vital to recognize them and take steps to deal with the issues as soon as possible. Conflict that is ignored or repressed does not go away: it simply festers, causing deep-seated resentments that are liable to explode at a later date. Ideally team members will be able to resolve their differences constructively on a one-to-one basis when difficulties first arise. This is more likely to happen in a climate of warmth and support (see pp.84–7).

Whenever team members encounter conflicts that they are unable to resolve themselves, encourage them to inform you. If necessary, arrange a meeting with the parties concerned with the explicit purpose of airing the problem and finding ways to resolve it. Give both sides the opportunity to express their feelings, listening without judgment or comment. Often the true facts will emerge after strong feelings have been expressed. Seek to identify the cause of the conflict by determining the underlying *needs* of both parties, as opposed to their expressed positions: conflicts usually occur when one person's attempts to reach a goal are blocked by another. With the benefit of a broader perspective, you may have a clearer understanding of the problem than those

involved. Drawing on your insights, help both parties to find practical and creative solutions that meet or even exceed both parties' needs, avoiding unsatisfactory compromises where possible.

If members start to get heated during this or any other team situation, it may be appropriate to impose a short break, or even adjourn the discussion until a later date. When such confrontations arise it is essential that you remain neutral throughout. Either party may attempt to enlist your support or even attack you. Resist the temptation to be drawn into the argument and try to remain calm at all times. Your example will encourage other team members to follow suit. If you are unable to remain neutral or are already involved in the conflict, it may be necessary to request a third party – someone respected by both sides – to act as mediator.

GROUPTHINK

In 1961, the presidency of the United States was surrounded by an aura of optimism, enthusiasm and energy. President Kennedy and his advisors had captured the idealism of many Americans with their commitment to civil rights and democracy. However, at the beginning of the presidency this group was responsible for one of the major foreign-policy fiascos of the decade: the support of the invasion of Cuba in the "Bay of Pigs" affair. Despite much intelligence information indicating the likely failure of such a venture, Kennedy and his advisors authorized the CIA to support Cuban exiles in an invasion. The attack was easily rebuffed and the exiles were taken prisoner or killed. Afterwards many commentators questioned how Kennedy and his advisors could have possibly imagined that the venture might be successful. Psychologists who analyzed the affair later concluded that a dangerous pattern of team processes was responsible, creating among Kennedy's cabinet an effect known as "groupthink".

First identified by the social psychologist Irving Janis in his study of failures in policy decisions, groupthink is a phenomenon whereby tightly-knit teams may err in their decision-making because they are more concerned with their own cohesiveness and unanimity than with the quality of the decisions made. Those who offer contrary views may be accused of disloyalty and prevented from expressing their ideas within the team. Groupthink is particularly likely to occur in teams with strong leaders who have a tendency to suppress dissent and to consistently state their own views at the beginning of team discussions.

Strong time pressures may serve as an additional factor, limiting the time available for team members to engage in a systematic search through the various options for appropriate solutions. Keen in any case to reach a quick decision, they insulate themselves from outside information and opinions, particularly those that go against the team view, and go with the first available option on which there is a consensus.

Encouraging participation (see pp.96–9) and constructive controversy (see pp.104–7) within your team are vital ways to counter the effects of groupthink. In addition, invite feedback from outsiders who are either affected by or knowledgeable about your team's work. For example, you could request customers to complete surveys, or ask other team managers to comment on their experiences. Do not use "devil's advocacy" to strengthen the majority view by testing its possible weaknesses: if you encourage artificial disagreement in this way, it lulls the group into a complacency that they are genuinely considering all sides of the argument. Guard against the tendency for your team to develop an "us" and "them" mentality with regard to other teams, as this encourages group conformity, which is conducive to groupthink. For example, if you hear team members stereotyping other teams as "incompetent" or "untrustworthy", counter their claims with evidence to the contrary.

SOCIAL LOAFING

In the 1890s a French agricultural engineer called Max Ringelmann explored whether individuals working alone were more effective than those working in teams. He instructed agricultural students to pull on a rope attached to a dynamometer (a devise for gauging energy expended) and measured the amount of pull. Working alone, the average student could pull a weight of 85 kg (191 lbs). Ringelmann then arranged the students into teams of seven and instructed them to pull on the rope as hard as possible. The average pull for a team of seven was 450 kg (1012 lbs). The teams were pulling only 75 per cent as hard as the aggregated work of seven individuals pulling alone.

The implication is that individuals work less hard when their efforts are combined with those of others than when they are working individually. This is a phenomenon psychologists call "social loafing". It may occur when a team member's contribution to the collective effort is difficult to identify and evaluate, and it challenges the common assumption that synergy is necessarily produced when individuals work together in groups. To prevent social loafing, you need to ensure that each member is fully committed to the work of the team and aware of the importance of his or her contribution. Distributing roles clearly and fairly, combined with a transparent monitoring system, will help you to do this. Further advice is given in Work Solution 19, opposite.

WORK SOLUTION 19

Maximizing effort

You can combat the problem of social loafing in a number of ways, all designed to ensure the healthy operation of the team as a collective enterprise in which each individual is thoroughly aware of, and proud of, their contribution.

1. Ensure that the team has a challenging and engaging task. If you think that the team is capable of more than it is currently doing, extend its ambition – for example, by tightening the numerical targets, or by adding tasks, in ways that contribute more to the organization.

2. Instill a sense of the critical value of each individual's contribution. Social loafing is most likely to occur when team members believe that their contributions to the team are dispensable. Ensure that roles are thoroughly explored in an initial negotiation and that the job descriptions that result are unambiguously clear (see pp.78–9).

3. Think of ways to heighten the interest of the most routine or repetitive work within the team – for example, collecting information can be more enjoyable if it is instantly fitted into a pre-determined system of classification.

4. Ensure that every team member's work is evaluated and that the results of the evaluation are made available to other team members. People have to feel not only that their work is indispensable but also that their performance is *visible* to other team members. For anyone who deals face-to-face with customers, for example, you should find a way to monitor the number of customers seen and the level of customer satisfaction.

DEFENSIVE ROUTINES

Like any organism, a team develops an immune system to fight threats to its stability. These defences are referred to as "defensive routines" and form part of the unspoken norms of the group. Norms are deeply embedded habits or ground-rules that govern the behaviour of team members. When new members join a team, they sense these unspoken codes of conduct and adjust their actions accordingly in order to fit in. Although evolved to protect the team, defensive routines are *negative* norms: they prevent teams from addressing the root-cause of their problems for the sake of preserving the cohesion of the group – a response that can dramatically inhibit team functioning.

Take the case of Martin, the leader of a team providing technical solutions to companies upgrading their IT systems. One of the key members of his team was Robert, a personal friend with a reputation as an outstanding project manager. Martin was convinced of Robert's value – he was managing three major projects and half the team members, as well as helping Martin with his heavy workload. Over the course of six months, Martin heard about a number of problems with clients but paid no attention to them, as both Robert and the team blamed the problems on customer incompetence. Then one day Martin discovered that a customer was threatening to cancel a major contract – a crisis that could damage the reputation of the company, as well as losing revenue. When Martin intervened he discovered that Robert had been managing the team ineffectively for some time, had repeatedly ignored customer feedback and was neglecting project

management. Here was a defensive routine in action. Because of Robert's reputation and special relationship with Martin, everybody, including Martin, had bought into the belief that he was doing a great job. The team had colluded in blaming outside agents – in this case, the customers – rather than confronting the uncomfortable issues of Robert's incompetence and Martin's misjudgment.

As this example shows, the problems concealed by defensive routines are often embarrassing, and so there is an unspoken agreement among the whole team not to discuss them, even potentially, as the results of team failings. The topic becomes a tacit taboo.

Exposing defensive routines is all the more difficult because of the unstated consensus that the team is immune from criticism. Unconscious fears may be at work: because the stone hides writhing problems, nobody dare lift it.

Teams are especially likely to show these symptoms within organizations that have a "blame culture". These are places where the reaction to failures, errors or near-misses is to search for somone to blame – to take responsibility for things going wrong. This is the opposite of a learning environment, where mistakes are meticulously analyzed in order to bring out the lessons inherent in them.

As manager, one way to minimize the pitfall of defence mechanisms is to treat all problems seriously, especially those that the team seems unable to resolve. Look beneath the surface rather than settling for superficial explanations. Question your own assumptions about the situation – without realizing it, you may be colluding in the defensive routine yourself. To expose a defensive routine takes courage, as it involves asking probing questions about the exact nature of the team's operations. If your questioning is met with automatic, uncritical resistance, that is all the more reason to explore further.

To guard against defensive routines you must also dismantle the blame cultures in which they arise. When diagnosing problems, make it clear that you are trying to find out What? rather than Who? And emphasize the importance of openness in any team that seeks to learn from its mistakes. Incorporate such openness in the team's list of values (see p.76) so it becomes a *positive* norm within the team.

WORK SOLUTION 20

Confronting defensive routines

When there is a problem in the team and you cannot confidently identify its cause, a defensive routine may be in operation. To address the issue, work through the following exercise during a meeting with team members.

1. Work with the team to clarify the nature of the problem – how it manifests itself, whom it affects, what its implications are. Ask each team member to suggest reasons why the problem might have occurred.

2. If you suspect a defensive routine, probe further with the team members. Ask them to work toward the underlying causes of the problem rather than the immediate causes. For example, apparent lack of cooperation by another team may be the immediate cause of a problem; communication failures within your team, and a fear of confronting those failures, may be the underlying causes.

3. For each problem, prompt team members to consider possible internal explanations (team actions or attitudes) as well as external explanations (actions or attitudes of others). Where necessary suggest alternative possibilities yourself. Praise team members who offer challenging ideas.

4. If people challenge the internal explanations, ask them to go through their reasoning. Explore all the possibilities, thoroughly probing below the surface. Still working with the team, try to see through the question of efficiency (doing things right) to the deeper question of effectiveness (doing the right things).

5. Once the source of the problem is revealed, explore the question, "How can we change the way we operate as a team to avoid this problem in the future?"

chapter 6

TEAMS AND THEIR ORGANIZATIONS

Teams do not exist in a vacuum. They operate within the wider context of an organization, and their success depends on their ability to work cooperatively with other teams and departments in the service of organizational goals.

The team manager is the vital link between the team and the organization. In this chapter we begin by looking generally at the process of change that occurs when an organization moves toward teamworking, and the role of the team manager in facilitating this process. Next we examine how the team manager can represent the team at a higher level within the organization – initiating change for the benefit of the team and the wider organization; intervening to gather the resources and support that the team needs to perform its task; and empowering the team to stand up for itself against ill-judged directives from those at a higher level. Finally we explore how the team manager can encourage the team to work cooperatively with other teams for the benefit of the whole organization.

MOVING TOWARD
TEAM-BASED WORKING

As we have seen, many organizations are increasingly looking to teams to help them meet the pressures of a competitive commercial climate. Examples include Fujitsu, IBM, Microsoft and Motorola. If your organization decides at the highest level to move toward teamworking, you may be asked to play an instrumental role in facilitating the change. To fulfill this role effectively you will need a clear understanding of the change process (see box, opposite).

Once the decision is taken to implement the change, you are likely to be involved in consultations to assess the structural and cultural adjustments needed to bring about teamworking. In such meetings there are four criteria you need to bear constantly in mind: the objectives of the organization; customer service (where applicable); innovation in products and/or services; and the effectiveness of teamworking. By repeating, mantra-like, the importance of these four elements, you can exert a positive influence on the organization's collective mentality.

The introduction of teamworking involves a major structural change. Replacing the vertical hierarchy of command is a planetary system: teams orbit around top management (themselves a team) like planets around a sun. The inspirational force of different teams affects the performance of the teams around them. Your role as a manager will be to ensure that your team works as a powerful and effective part of that solar system, and that you think in terms of how the system as a whole works, not just your particular planet.

Gently but persistently work to get your managerial colleagues to reduce the number of vertical levels in the organization: across, say, sixty staff, three levels is probably the maximum reduction you will be able to achieve.

Think carefully about the implications of the proposed change. How will current systems need to be revised? What

SIX STEPS TO TEAM-BASED WORKING

Although the process of transition to team-based working will vary between organizations, it is possible to identify six basic stages:

1. Deciding to team: Top management decide whether to implement teams by considering the performance challenges faced by the organization and the best structure for meeting these challenges.

2. Planning: Top management conduct a review to establish the structural and cultural changes needed to bring about team-based working. This process may involve consultations with managers further down the organizational hierarchy. Based on this review, a plan for implementing the changes is formulated and a steering team set up to put the plan into action.

3. Briefing: Employees at all levels are briefed on all aspects of the change process and their role within that process.

4. Developing supports: The steering team coordinates the establishment of systems necessary for effective teamworking, such as communication networks, training programs and reward systems.

5. Establishing teams: The steering team works with managers to organize employees into teams and get them up and running. If a large number of teams is involved, this process may take place in phases.

6. Reviewing teamworking: Once teams are established, managers are required to monitor their team's development, implement changes to improve performance and evaluate the contribution of their team to organizational goals (see p.141). This information enables top management to assess the success of the move to teamworking.

support will you and your colleagues require to develop the teamworking skills? Discuss these issues with other managers, as well as those you manage, to find out their views. Then represent your thoughts to the appropriate senior forum.

Working with the information supplied by you and other managers, those implementing the change should formulate a concrete strategy detailing each phase in the process, the time-frame, and the resources required to drive the change through. During the briefing phase you will be required to communicate the specific details of the change process to those who will report to you. As well as addressing practicalities, you will need to gain the support of employees by explaining the benefits of teamworking. Acknowledge that the process will not be easy, but present the difficulties as challenges rather than obstacles. Expect to encounter some resistance. Break it down by listening to what people say and taking a supportive but constructive approach to any anxieties.

Work cooperatively with the steering team and other

managers to develop and implement the systems appropriate to teamworking. It will be up to you to get your own team up and running. During the initial stages, hold regular reviews of your team's performance and initiate meetings with other managers to share your experiences.

WORK SOLUTION 21

Evaluating teamworking

As part of the transition toward a team-based organization, it is vital to ask whether this structure is producing the intended results. To do so, you and other managers in your company should use the following questions to evaluate the effectiveness of your teams in terms of their contribution to the organization. Senior management will be able to use the responses you feed back to them to gain a clearer picture of the success of the shift toward teamworking and the areas that need further work.

1. What contribution does my team make to the attainment of organizational goals? (Give concrete examples.)

2. What role does my team play in producing more positive customer experiences? (Give evidence.)

3. How does my team contribute to improving business processes and reducing the cycle-time for producing products or delivering services?

4. What changes in products and/or ways of working has my team introduced?

5. To what extent are team members developing their skills in the directions they wish for and in ways that enhance the organization's ability to meet its objectives?

6. To what extent has team-based working led to an increase in employee satisfaction and a decrease in employee stress?

7. To what extent do I regard the shift toward a team-based structure as successful and why? What could be done to make it more successful?

INITIATING CHANGE

As well as implementing decisions imposed from above, there may be changes that you and your team seek to initiate. These could range from small-scale system changes, such as the installation of more efficient software in your department, to much more radical structural changes, such as reducing the number of management levels in the organization. How should you go about effecting such changes?

The initiation of any change usually involves the use of persuasion strategies to convince people that the change would benefit the organization. However, if your views are in the minority, or go against the opinions of senior management, you are unlikely to succeed on your own – and in extreme circumstances you may even find yourself rejected from the organization altogether. The solution is to involve others in your drive for change. As feminist and environmental groups have demonstrated, when a persistent, vocal and passionate minority argues repeatedly for change, this often leads to a shift in the attitudes of the majority. People exposed to such a minority are forced to think more creatively around the issues and, as a result, are likely to make better-quality decisions and to arrive at judgments independent of the majority view or status quo.

Talk about your ideas for change with colleagues. You may find that they share your views and have additional ideas of their own. If you band together to form a highly committed change team (see Work Solution 22, opposite), the power of your individual voices will be greatly amplified and senior management will no longer be able to ignore you.

WORK SOLUTION 22

Forming a change team

Forming a change team is a realistic first step toward introducing changes into your organization, whatever your place in the hierarchy. The success of this team (as for any team) depends on creating a powerful vision and strategy to which all members are committed. When these are in place, the team will act passionately and determinedly to influence the views and orientations of others within the organization. The following exercise takes you through the process of forming your change team:

1. Bring together a team of no more than six to eight people who share your ideas and are prepared to invest time in initiating these changes.

2. Arrange for the team to spend at least a day together developing a clear vision of what you intend to accomplish. This vision should be concrete, coherent and inspiring, and should have the commitment of all team members. Discuss the potential values and benefits of introducing the change into the organization. Develop these into a cogent case for change, expressed as a series of bullet points.

3. At a subsequent meeting, develop a plan describing the steps the team will take to present its proposal persistently and repeatedly to the rest of the organization. To do this, first identify the primary targets for your proposals: these are likely to be senior managers or other influential individuals, who may be sympathetic to the changes. Decide who will approach the targets and how they will do it. Also incorporate into the plan consultation processes involving other organizational members in order to anticipate and deal with conflicts that may arise from the initiative. Set a date for a follow-up meeting to report back to the team on the progress of the plan.

SEEKING ORGANIZATIONAL SUPPORT

For your team to function most effectively it is vital that team members feel that their work is supported and valued, not only by you but also by the wider organization. Just as it is part of your role to create a climate in which your team can flourish, so too it is your responsibility to monitor the organizational support offered to your team and take remedial steps when it falls short.

Begin by ensuring that your team has sufficient resources to carry out its tasks. If resources are lacking, negotiate with senior management on your team's behalf. Communicate the needs of your team, the basis for these needs, and the impact for the team if these needs are not met. Emphasize the benefits to the organization if your request is granted.

Effective training systems also form a vital part of organizational support. Because of the cross-functional nature of teams, members require a diverse range of skills. Where skills (particularly those related specifically to teamworking) are lacking, it is important that your organization can offer suit-

able training in forms such as courses, seminars, paid study-leave and mentoring programs (whereby more senior or experienced individuals provide support and guidance to less experienced colleagues). Your team might also benefit from process support whereby someone in your organization (or an external consultant) is on hand to assist people when they have difficulties that you are unable to solve.

If you feel that the current training and support systems in your organization fail to cater for your team's needs, attempt to initiate change. First identify what improvements could be made by discussing the issue with other team managers and exploring the approaches of other organizations. Then seek to implement those changes by negotiating with appropriate senior managers. If this approach fails, adopt other change strategies outlined on pp.142–3.

Verbal as well as practical support from the organization will do much to boost your team's morale, motivation and performance. Ensure that others are aware of the good work your team is doing by broadcasting team and individual successes verbally, via email, or in the company newsletter. Moreover, inform team members of the positive things senior managers and others have said about the team and encourage senior managers to pass on their praise personally.

Conversely, when you hear of managers speaking derogatively about the team, arrange to meet with them to discuss the issue. Do this in a genuine spirit of enquiry, not aggressively. Explain that your motivation is to ensure the effective functioning of your team and the organization overall. Investigate the basis for the remarks. If valid, they can provide valuable feedback. If not, your direct approach will signal that people should be careful not to make negative remarks without basis. By pursuing this strategy consistently, you will find others come to treat your team with the respect it deserves.

EMPOWERING YOUR TEAM

Teams are a vital source of innovation within organizations, helping them to adapt to a fast-paced commercial world. However, to reap these benefits organizations must empower their teams, giving them not only the resources they need to carry out their tasks independently, but also the opportunity to contribute their ideas to the running of the business.

As team manager there is much that you can do to empower your team. In addition to representing the needs of your team (see pp.144–5), you should also stand up for your team when the direction from the top seems unwise. Neither you nor your team should assume that those at a senior level necessarily know better than you do. Because the team operates at a grass-roots level, members may have access to information that senior managers do not.

Rather than challenging the decisions of senior management outright, gently question the basis for their opinions and supply any information that might lead to different conclusions. If you are told not to question the decisions of senior management, explain that you simply wish to enhance the effectiveness and creativity of the organization. Persist in raising your concerns and seek support from other team managers. If you and your colleagues raise the issue collectively, senior management are more likely to pay attention.

This pushing back at the organization should take place in the context of lots of positive messages from you and your team about the good things senior managers are doing. Constructive suggestions are likely to be more welcome when delivered in a context of support, praise and enthusiasm.

When team members see that you take their concerns seriously and are willing to represent them to the rest of the organization, they will experience a greater sense of control over their work. Instead of feeling helpless in the face of organizational weaknesses, they are more likely to suggest creative alternatives, thereby forging the path to change.

To support this dynamic, set up meetings in which team members can communicate their opinions to senior managers directly. Discuss the issues with your team beforehand. Try to reach a consensus of opinion so that the team presents a united front. Encourage members to acknowledge what has gone right as well as what has gone wrong when raising problems. For example, a member of a sales team may report that the company's investment in high-tech presentation equipment has allowed the team to increase sales, but point out that failure to deliver goods on time has led to orders being cancelled. Such an approach is more likely to lead to a receptive response from senior managers. Where possible, demonstrate your support for your team by echoing their concerns. This will boost members' confidence and encourage senior managers to take your team seriously.

A fundamental weakness in many team-based organizations is the rivalry and subsequent hostility that often develops between teams. The tendency to discriminate to the advantage of our own group and to discriminate against members of other groups is an evolutionary hangover from our tribal past. In the context of a modern organization, this instinct is inappropriate and often damaging. Unlike our tribal ancestors, who often had to compete for limited resources, the teams in an organization share the same interest – the efficacy of the organization as a whole. If your organization is to be successful, it is vital to recognize the tribal instinct within your team so that you can take steps to pre-empt it.

The tribal instinct is activated by threats (or perceived threats) from other teams. For example, a creative team may experience a symbolic threat to its goals and values when a finance team imposes budgetary restraints that force the creative team to compromise its artistic integrity. Similarly, two product-development teams may feel threatened by each

other because they are competing for resources. Threats such as these often lead to prejudice, which can manifest itself as anger, resentment, stereotyping and a desire to undermine the other teams.

If you recognize these negative attitudes and actions developing among your team, resist the temptation to buy into them. Listen calmly to members' grievances. If you feel that the grievances are based on little more than blind prejudice, ask members to put themselves in the position of the other team. This encourages empathy, giving your team a different perspective and helping them to view the other team as a group of individuals like themselves. Point out that although hostility toward other teams is a natural human tendency, it is damaging to the teams concerned and the organization as a whole. As an alternative, suggest ways of addressing and solving the problems that are causing members to be negative in their comments.

If your team has a legitimate grievance, you should approach the team manager of the other team. Without apportioning blame, explain your team's point of view, then ask your colleague to give the perspective of his or her team. Respond by emphasizing that you understand the position of your colleague's team and that you would like to work with them to find a solution that is satisfactory to both sides.

Most problems can be resolved by increasing levels of trust and understanding between teams. For example, taking a risk with another team demonstrates that you trust them and encourages them to reciprocate. A wire and cable company used this approach to resolve a longstanding conflict between the production and quality teams. The production team resented what they saw as the excessive checking, control and criticism of their work by the quality team. To improve relations the quality team manager suggested that the production team take responsibility for checking and improving their own work without the involvement of the quality team. The quality department would simply offer support for tackling problems that the production team had difficulty solving. This demonstration of trust in the production team dramatically improved relations between the teams. Rather than battling with each other, they became partners in the drive to improve performance, which ultimately led to a fall in complaints from customers about poor-quality goods.

Altruistic gestures have a similarly positive effect by demonstrating goodwill toward other teams. In one case a research and development team had used up its staffing budget before the end of the year, but wanted to keep on a particularly promising temporary worker and employ her permanently the following year. To help them out, a "rival" team with a staff-budget surplus offered to hire the person, giving 80 per cent of the worker's time to the first team. In the short term, both teams benefited from the valuable experience of the temporary worker, and in the long term the goodwill created by the gesture provided the basis for a positive relationship between the teams that lasted for years.

Encouraging your team to identify and value the differences between teams can help to reduce divisions caused by competition and rivalry. When team members are secure in the knowledge that they have a unique contribution to make to the organization, they will feel more inclined to cooperate with other teams. You can promote better understanding between teams by organizing exchanges in which members work in other teams for a short period or visit as observers.

WORK SOLUTION 23

Lowering the drawbridge

If your team wants to gain the trust and support of other teams, it must first open up to them. One way to do this is to write lucid reports summarizing the information and learning acquired by your team during the course of its work so that everyone within the organization can benefit. If your team works on specific projects, the obvious time to produce such a report is upon completion of the project. If the work of your team is ongoing, compile a report from every six months to once a year. Not only will this benefit other teams, but it will also help your team to consolidate and become consciously aware of what it has learned during the course of teamworking.

1. Begin the report with a general section describing the specific goals and overall direction of the team, and a summary of the progress of the team's work during the project (or since the last report if the work is ongoing). Consult with team members to ensure that they accord with your view of team events. Where there is disagreement, make any necessary modifications.

2. Ask each team member (and do this yourself as well) to write a brief personal report detailing the following: new ways of working that he/she, or the team as a whole, has developed; problems that arose and how these were resolved; mistakes that were made and the learning gained from them. Place these personal testimonies in the report after the general overview and conclude with an evaluation of the team's success in terms of its original goals.

3. Make this report available to the rest of the company so that they can benefit from the learning of your team. Posting it on an intranet or web forum where everyone in the company can access it, regardless of geographical location, is ideal. Alternatively, print out some hard copies and give them to your fellow team managers, who can then share the information with their teams.

REFLEXIVITY: THE KEY TO TEAM SUCCESS

As human beings we are blessed with the capacity to consciously reflect on and learn from our experience. As we have seen repeatedly throughout this book, it is in this unique ability that we find the key to team success. By reflecting on their experiences of working together, teams can identify what works for them and what doesn't. They can then use this information to improve performance by doing more of what works and less of what doesn't. For this reason, teams that actively take time out to reflect on what they are doing are more effective than those that do not, be they coal-mining teams, television production teams or management teams.

For this reason it is crucial to encourage your team to set aside time periodically for reflection. At each session, ask them to clarify what it is they are trying to achieve and assess how they are going about it. Then discuss any changes that should be made and formulate a plan to implement them. At the next session, ensure that this plan has been carried out, then begin the process again. This three-step process of reflection, planning and action is reflexivity – the heart of good teamwork.

In addition to organizing regular reflection meetings, encourage your team to cultivate ongoing self-awareness by constantly asking "What can we learn from this?" Answering this question on a regular basis will concentrate your team on their long-term goals as well as encouraging members to take responsibility for their own and fellow members' development. Successes as well as failures provide ideal cues for such reflection. In addition to celebrating, take time to consciously

consider the reasons behind each success. This will help the team to replicate those conditions again in the future.

You can apply reflexivity to any team process. For example, if member activities make it difficult to arrange meetings, the team should spend time discussing what team or individual processes are getting in the way and how the team can resolve these issues. Similarly, if members feel overloaded with work, the team should reflect on its objectives and priorities, and how it is currently functioning in relation to these, by asking questions such as "Why are we so overloaded?", "What should be taking priority, given our objectives and customer needs?", "Why is our work not fun?" and "How can we achieve our objectives but feel less pressured and anxious?" The building blocks of a better future for your team lie in the answers to such questions.

Amabile, T. M. *Motivating creativity in organizations: On doing what you love and loving what you do,* California Management Review 40, 39–58, 1997

Belbin, R. M. *Team roles at work: A strategy for human resource management,* Butterworth, Heinemann (Oxford), 1993

Brown, R. *Group processes (2nd Edition),* Blackwell (Oxford), 2000

Edelmann, R. *Interpersonal conflicts at work,* British Psychological Society (Leicester), 1993

Fisher, R., Ury, W. & Patton, B. *Getting to yes: Negotiating an agreement without giving in,* Random House (London), 1999

Flood, P., MacCurtain, S. & West, M. A. *Effective top management teams,* Blackhall Press (Dublin, Ireland), 2001

Fontana, D. *Managing stress,* Blackwell (Oxford), 1989

Goleman, D. *Emotional intelligence: Why it can matter more than IQ,* Bloomsbury (London), 1995

Goleman, D., Boyatzis, R. & McKee, A. *The new leaders: Transforming the art of leadership into the science of results,* Little, Brown (London), 2002

Hackman, J. R. (Ed) *Leading teams: Setting the stage for great performances,* Harvard Business School Press (Harvard, USA), 2002

Hackman, J. R. (Ed) *Groups that work (and those that don't): Conditions for effective teamwork,* Jossey Bass (San Francisco), 1990

Mohrman, S., Cohen, S. & Mohrman, L. *Designing team-based organizations,* Jossey Bass (London), 1995

Parker, G., McAdams, J. & Zielinski, D. *Rewarding teams: Lessons from the trenches,* Jossey Bass (San Francisco), 2000

Seligman, M. E. P. *Learned optimism: How to change your mind and your life,* Pocket Books (London), 1998

Tjosvold, D. *Team organization: An enduring competitive advantage,* John Wiley and Sons (Chichester, UK), 1991

West, M. A. & Markiewicz, L. *Building team-based working: A practical guide to organizational transformation,* Blackwell/British Psychological Society (Oxford), 2003

West, M. A. *Developing creativity in organizations,* Blackwell/British Psychological Society (Oxford), 1996

West, M. A. *Effective teamwork: Practical lessons from organizational research,* Blackwell/British Psychological Society (Oxford), 2003

Yukl, G. *Leadership in organizations (4th Edition),* Prentice Hall (London), 1998

INDEX

A

action teams 25, 73
active listening 52–4
advertising jobs 70
advice teams 25
affirmations 59
agendas 94, 95
aggression 44–5, 48
airline crews 25
alienation 12–13, 14–15
anger 44–5, 51, 56
anxiety 44–5
appraisal 112–15, 131
 and rewards 116–18, 119
 see also reviews
appraisal support 84, 86
approach (to team
 management) 26–7
assembly teams 24
assertiveness 48–9
assessment 23
 see also appraisal
atmosphere 84, 86–7
autonomy, team 122

B

Bay of Pigs 128
Bandura, Albert 47
Belbin, Dr R. Meredith 85
benefits of teams
 for organizations 16–17
 for individuals 18
belonging, sense of 12, 15
"Big Five" model of
 personality 72
blame culture 134
body language 53, 56, 57, 82
bonding, team 20, 76
brainstorming 101–102, 107
breathing (for relaxation) 41, 44

bridging (between teams) *see*
 cooperation
budgets 109

C

car manufacture 13
change 17, 138–43
charisma 26, 29–30, 58
coaching 26–7, 28, 30, 65,
 84–6, 87, 125
coaching skill-sets 31, 43
co-ordinator (classification of
 Dr R. Meredith Belbin) 85
collaboration (between teams)
 149–50
commitment, work 15, 18,
 96, 130
communication 12, 21, 30,
 48, 52–7, 80–83, 125
 between teams 123
 concerning problems
 44–5, 48–9
 and decision-making 98,
 104–106
 modes of 81–2, 94
 non-verbal 53, 56, 57, 82
 skills 21, 52–7, 98
 team lifespan and 24–5
 see also feedback
compassion *see* empathy
competencies, of teams 20, 23
competition
 between teams 148
 within teams 105–6, 116–17
competitors 90
completer finisher
 (classification of Dr R.
 Meredith Belbin) 85
compliments 42
 see also feedback

conflict 22, 124–7
 between teams 123
 communication,
 concerning 44–5, 48–9
 positive aspects 68, 69, 126
 team lifespan and 24–5
 resolution 22, 126–7
construction teams 24
constructive controversy
 105–107, 129
contingency plans 110, 111
cooperation 12, 84, 104
 between teams 148–51
creativity 17, 21, 41, 113
 debate and 21–2
 facilitating team 123
 in problem-solving
 100–103
criticism 42
 see also feedback
cultural backgrounds 67–8
customers 90
customer service 138

D

debate *see* discussions
decision-making 16, 22, 96,
 98, 104–107, 128–9
 pressure and 128–9
 step-ladder debating
 exercise 99
 see also meetings
defensive routines 132–5
delegating/dumping/
 deferring 34
democracy, in teamwork 96–7
departmental teams 24
development teams 24–5
developmental stages (of
 teams) 64–5, 69

difficult people 49, 97, 124–5
disagreement *see* conflict
discussions/debate 21–2,
  101–102, 105–106
  step-ladder debating
    exercise 99
diversity 21–2, 66, 67–9, 126
  problems of 68–9, 124
dominance 96–7
dominant people 73, 97

E

effectiveness (of teams) 16,
  38, 73, 88, 130
electrical-repair teams 25
email 81–2, 94
emotional climate 38–40, 84,
  86–7
emotional support 84, 86
emotions
  assessing and dealing with
    38–40, 44–5, 50–51, 57
  negative 44–5, 51
  positive 26, 46–7, 59–60
  thoughts and 46–7
empathy 30, 40, 50–51, 57
empowerment 18, 98, 146–7
evaluation 20–23, 78, 130,
  131, 141
  see also appraisal *and*
    reflection
evolution 8, 12, 15, 148
Extraversion-Introversion
  (scale of Myers Briggs Type
    Indicator) 72
eye contact 54

F

factories 12–14, 16–17
failure, causes of 122–3

fairness 26, 87, 116–17
favouritism 87
feedback 22, 23, 42–3, 81,
  129, 145
  individual sessions 97,
    114–15
  responding to 42, 43
  see also appraisals and
    reports
feelings *see* emotions
financial performance 17
fire-fighting units 73
flexibility, organizational 14
flight-deck crews 25
Ford, Henry 13
forming (stage in team
  development) 64
frustration 40, 44, 51, 56,
  122
Fujitsu 138

G

gender balance 67
goals see objectives
goal-setting (exercise) 115
groundrules 65, 76, 77, 82
groupthink 104–105, 128–9

H

health-care teams 24
hidden profile phenomenon
  101
history (of teams) 8, 10,
  12–14, 15, 148
"home team" 87
hostility (toward other teams)
  149
human resources departments
  70
humour 47, 56, 76

I

IBM 138
identity 74
  team identity 74–9
  see also self
implementer (classification of
  Dr R. Meredith Belbin) 85
impression management 98
in-groups 85, 87
incentives *see* reward(s)
individuals
  appraisals 114–15
  benefits of teams for 18
  difficult 49, 97, 124–5
  rewarding *see* reward(s)
Industrial Revolution 12–13
inflexibility, organizational
  13
influence 38–9, 58–61
  see also persuasion *and*
    power
information 80–82, 94
  displaying 108, 151
  gathering 43
  and problem-solving
    100–101
  processing 83
  sharing 22
  see also feedback
informational support 84,
  86
innovation 17, 113, 138
instrumental (practical)
  support 84, 86
interpersonal problems *see*
  conflict
interviewing 67, 70–71
introspection 39–40, 42
  see also meditation
involvement teams 25

J

Janis, Irving 128
Japan and Japanese working
  methods 14
jargon 76
jealousy 87
jokes 47, 76
Judging-Perceiving (scale of
  Myers Briggs Type
    Indicator) 72

K

Kennedy, President John F. 128

L

laughter 47, 56, 76
leading/leadership 28, 29–30,
  31
leadership skill-sets 31, 43
learning 17, 18, 30, 152
learning environment 134
legal teams 25
listening 52–4
loafing, social 130

M

maintenance teams 24
management
  managing 28–9, 31
  senior see senior
    management
  styles of 26–8, 122–3
  time see time management
  see also team managers/
    management
management skill-sets 31, 43
mass production 12–15, 16–17
meaning, finding 74
mediation 127
meditation 41, 59

see also introspection
meetings 22, 78, 94–8
  between teams and senior
    management 147
  chairing 60, 94
  concerning change 140
  conflict resolution 126–7
  exercises for 77, 83, 85, 99,
    135, 153
  facilitating 22, 94
  managing 94–5
  power and 60
  review 78, 140
  and support 86
mental focus 38–40, 41
Microsoft 138
mindfulness 41
mining teams 24
minutes 94
mirroring, body language 57
modelling 26, 29, 51, 68, 82,
  86, 142
monitor evaluator
  (classification of Dr R.
    Meredith Belbin) 85
monitoring systems 130, 131
  see also appraisals
motivation 15, 96, 119
Motorola 138
multiculturalism 67–8
Myers Briggs Type
  Indicator 72

N

negative emotions 44–5
negotiation teams 25
networking 58–60
new technologies 110
non-verbal communication
  53, 56, 57, 82

non-work activities 76
norming (stage in team
  development) 65, 69
norms 65, 76, 77, 82, 86, 132
  negative 132
  positive 134
  see also defensive routines
nuclear power station teams 73

O

objectives 91–3
  appropriateness for teams
    19
  feedback and 43
  importance of sharing
    12, 15
  individual and team 20,
    78, 114, 115, 131
  measuring 112
  setting 92, 93, 114–15, 131
  timing of formulation 92
  see also vision
open-door policy 86
openness 50–51, 54, 102, 134
  in reward systems 116–18
optimism 26
  see also positive thinking
organizations
  change 17
  individuals and 18
  problems of 12–15
  size and flexibility of 13–14
  support for teams 144–5
  teams and 136–51; see also
    teams, relationships with
    other teams
  see also senior
    management
out-groups 87
outward-bound activities 69

P

panic 44
participation 96–9, 129
passive-aggression 48
passivity 48
pay 119
performance
    beliefs and 47
    and team cohesion 73
performance measures
    112–15, 117
performing (stage in team
    development) 65
perks 86–7
personality 72–3
persuasion 61, 142
planning 22, 35–7, 108–11
    see also preparation
plant (classification of Dr R.
    Meredith Belbin) 85
politics 58
positive thinking 26, 46–7,
    59–60
power 58–60, 96–7
practical (instrumental)
    support 84, 86
prehistory 8, 10, 15, 148
preparation
    for meetings 94
    see also planning
presentations 55
pressure 34, 129
    see also stress *and* time
        management
priorities 34–7
    see also time management
problems
    communication
        concerning 44–5,
        48–9

    exploration and solving
        46–7, 100–107, 135
    need to reveal 51
    need to treat seriously
        134
    see also conflict
processing information 83
production methods 12–13,
    14–15, 16–17
production teams 24
productivity 15
project teams 24–5
project triangle 109–10
prophecies, self-fulfilling
    46–7
psychometric tests 72
punishment 26

Q

quality 17, 149–50
quality circles 18, 25
questionnaires 23, 31
    for formal feedback 43
    for team competencies 23
    for team management 31
    personality assessment 72
questions for interviews 71

R

recruitment 66–7, 70–71
referent power 59–60
reflection 39–41, 42, 152–3
    see also meditation
reflective listening 54
reframing (events/problems)
    46, 101–102
relationships
    between teams *see* under
        teams
    communication and 52

    effectiveness and 73
    self-awareness and 40
relaxation 41
reports, publishing 151
    see also feedback
research teams 24–5
resonance, emotional 50, 51
resource investigator
    (classification of Dr R.
    Meredith Belbin) 85
resources 59, 108
respect 105
responsibility 34, 36
    need for understanding of
        25, 125
    power and 59–60
    within teams 78–9, 80, 96,
        131
résumés 66–7, 70
reviews *see* appraisal,
    evaluation, meetings *and*
    reflection
reward(s) 26, 86–7, 105–106,
    116–19
    individual/team 116–19,
        123
    optimizing 119
Ringelmann, Max 130
risk 20, 110, 149
risk management 108–11
risky shift 105
rivalry 87, 148
role modelling 26, 29
roles 12, 13, 18, 78–9, 80
    need for understanding of
        25, 125
    and objectives 131
    of team managers 24–5,
        28–30, 64
rules *see* groundrules

S

safety 110
  see also support
sales teams 24, 119
scapegoating 124
scheduling 108–109
  see also time management
selection/recruitment 66–8,
  70–71
self, sense of 39
self-assessment and self-
  reflection 23, 31, 34–7, 88,
  134
self-awareness 38–40, 41, 42
self-belief 47, 59
self-fulfilling prophecies 46–7
self-management 32–61
senior management 60, 142,
  146
  see also organizations
Sensing-Intuition
  (scale of Myers Briggs Type
  Indicator) 72
service teams 24
shaper (classification of Dr R.
  Meredith Belbin) 85
shyness 97–8
social bonds 20, 76, 82, 86, 87
social functions 76, 82, 86, 87
social loafing 130–31
software development teams
  24–5
solitary reflection 39
speaking 54–6
  see also communication
specialist (classification of Dr
  R. Meredith Belbin) 85
sponsors 90
sport 76
sports teams 20, 28

stability, team 87
staff-involvement groups 25
stakeholders and stakeholder
  analysis 90, 103
storming (stage in team
  development) 64–5, 69
stress 18, 34
  see also pressure
success
  beliefs and 47
  and team identity 28, 76,
    152–3
support 18, 20, 26–7, 30,
  84–7, 123
  for difficult individuals 125
  organizational 144–5
  time for 36, 84, 86
  types 84
surgical teams 25

T

targets *see* objectives
tasks
  appropriateness for teams
    19, 122
  delegating/dumping/
    deferring 34, 36
  and roles/responsibilities
    78–9
  urgent/important 34–7
team appraisals 112–14
team building 62, 66–87
  exercises 69, 77, 83, 85, 99,
    131, 135, 151
team formation 30, 64
team identity 74–7
team managers/management
  26–31
  coaching 28, 30, 31
  in meetings 22, 94–8

leading 28, 29–30, 31
  managing 28–9, 31
  management styles 26–8,
    122–3
  questionnaire concerning
    31
  roles at different stages
    64–5
  roles in different types of
    teams 24–5
  self-management 32–61
  time management 34–7
team meetings *see* meetings
teams
  balance in 66–9, 70, 72, 73
  competencies of 20–23
  competition within 65,
    105–106, 116–17
  definition 12
  disbanding 25, 152–3
  diversity 21
  exchanges between 150
  history of 8, 12–15
  identity-building 74–7
  involving present members
    in interviewing 70–71
  lifespan 24–5
  membership 21, 66–9, 70
  problems 49, 120–35
  reflexivity 152–3
  relationships with other
    teams 113, 123, 129, 136,
    148–51
  and responsibility 78–9,
    80, 96, 122, 130–31
  rewarding *see* reward(s)
  setting objectives 91–3; *see
    also* objectives
  skills of 20–23
  social aspects 20, 76, 86, 87

stabilizing 87
stages of development 64–5, 69
tasks appropriate for 19
types of 24–5
viability of 112–13
teamworker (classification of Dr R. Meredith Belbin) 85
teamworking
  benefits 14, 16–18
  changing to 138–41
  steps to 139
  trend toward 138
teasing 47
Thinking–Feeling (scale of Myers Briggs Type Indicator) 72
thoughts, emotions and 46–7

threats (from other teams) 148
time management 34–7, 39–40
  journals 35–6, 37
  see also scheduling
time pressure 28, 35, 108, 129
timescales 109
timidity 97–8
training 144, 145
transactional approach to management 26–8
transformational approach to management 26–8
trust (between teams) 149–51
two-way relationships 85
types (of teams) 24–5

V
values 74–7
  importance of sharing 124
  linked to rewards 118, 119
  viability of 112–13
vision 90–91, 112
  identification with 20
  see also objectives
vision statements 90–91, 93
voting 96

W
win–lose mentality 106
win–win culture 106
work loads 22, 78, 153
working methods 14–15
working parties 25

ACKNOWLEDGMENTS

Thanks to my team from whom so much of the knowledge in this book emanates: Judy Scully, Gary Fisher, Carol Borrill, Jeremy Dawson, Pat Clark and Basia Nowakowska. And thanks to Lucy Latchmore at Duncan Baird for her editorial contributions to the book and her determination to ensure a completed and accessible guide for team managers.

If you would like to offer suggestions for developing ways of leading teams to success, share your experiences of leading teams, or if you or your organization require further information about my work with teams and organizations, I would be very pleased if you would contact me at: almalane@ftech.co.uk.